The Other Side of a

Glock

The riveting tales from the life adventures of retired

police officer, Jim Flygare

by

Sherry Allred

Sherry Allred

©2015 by Sherry Allred

The Other Side of a Glock

Text Copyright © 2015 by Sherry Allred.

Cover and Design Copyright © 2015 by Rachel Allred

Cover by Rachel Allred

Design by Rachel Allred and Sherry Allred

All rights reserved. Printed in the United States. No part of this book may be reproduced in any form or by any electronic or mechanical means without permission in writing by the publisher. Published by Sherry Allred. Centerville, Utah, 2015. You may contact the publisher through **www.sherryallred.com**.

The following account contains true stories of retired police officer, Jim Flygare, which occurred during his 20 years of service as a Public Safety Worker. Some of the names and character descriptions have been changed to respect the confidences of those involved in the incidences as well as to protect Jim's family from any retaliations that might occur from family members of criminals Jim had confrontations with. If any names, places or events in this book are similar to other events that took place outside of Jim Flygare's experiences, they are strictly coincidental. Some details and dialogue were added to assist in the story flow but all events and emotions involved are true as recorded from the words of Jim Flygare.

Other books by Sherry Allred:

Corvette: The Courage of a Cowboy

Andragathia

Clarence Moon

For further information, please visit: www.sherryallred.com

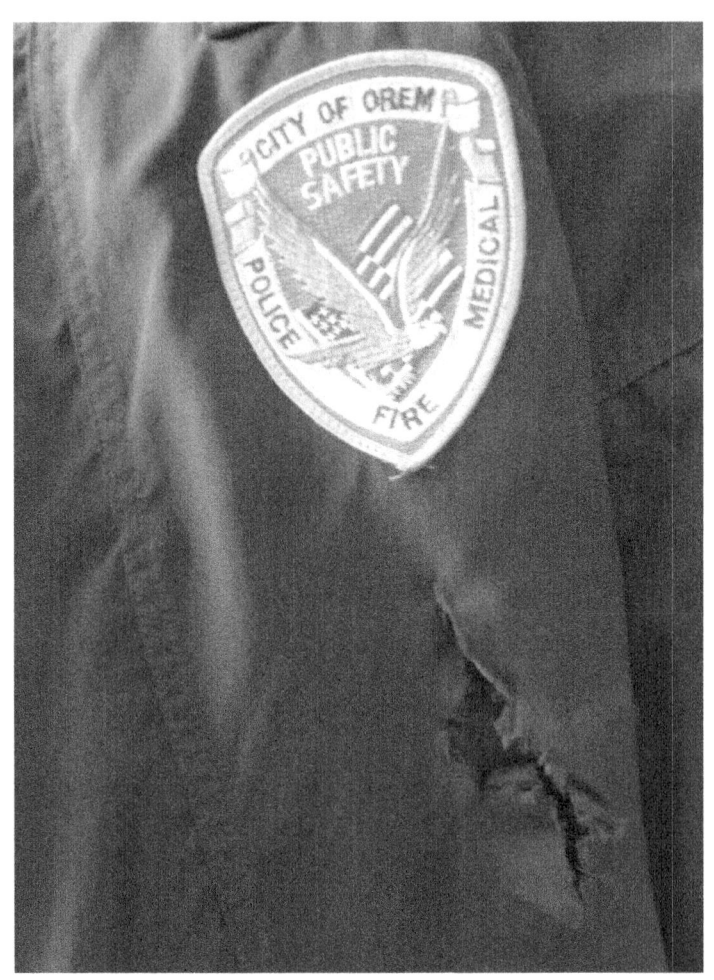

"Woe unto them that call evil good, and good evil; that put darkness for light, and light for darkness..."

-Isaiah 5:20 *(King James Bible "Authorized Version")*

PREFACE

JIM'S ROLE

With bullets suddenly surging past his face, Officer Jim Flygare's mind quickly shifted into defense mode. Staring back at the muzzle of a Russian Makarov 9mm pistol, he instinctively dodged the gun's deadly ware. Jim shot back as the assailant relentlessly continued to fire. Fully engaged, Jim hardly noticed the smell or even the taste of the gun powder as it permeated the air. He didn't feel the pain in his arm as the blast tore through the sleeve of his police jacket. He just focused on what he'd been trained to do: *protect*.

The Other Side of a Glock reveals the riveting and true adventures of retired police officer, Jim Flygare. For 20 years, he served the citizens of Utah County, facing life-threatening situations, listening to troubled victims, counseling traumatized witnesses of graphic scenes, and saving countless lives. He encountered many unusual events, experienced unforeseen emotions, and witnessed many miracles.

Jim dreamed of being a police officer, with all its challenges and intrigue. Even though he understood the risks it entailed, he had the courage to wear the uniform and the vision to see past his own safety to protect the security and lifestyle of others.

A RISING CONTROVERSY

Jim, like all other police officers, was trained to perform his duties with the intention of keeping the public safe, despite the perilous encounters and emotional setbacks he might endure. Twenty years before Jim retired, he took on his career whole-heartedly. But things have changed since he first entered the police academy. In addition to low pay and on-the-job hazards, a new challenge has emerged with the increase of public scrutiny, making it even more difficult for a police officer to fulfill his responsibilities. It has even discouraged the number of new recruits applying for positions within the profession. Matter of fact, the issue is becoming so heated throughout the nation, that if the problem isn't resolved soon, its course will be irreversible and its repercussions will adversely impact every group, race, organization, social classification, religion, gender, and age.

In the past few years, police officers have taken the center ring of interrogation under harsh societal scrutiny, especially when a shooting involving a police officer has occurred. Lately, cities have violently revolted in riotous actions due to misunderstandings and incorrect suppositions. The battle between good and evil has nearly become a spectator event as society has stood on the side lines arguing whether the police officer is the good guy or the bad guy. Our nation's security is becoming at risk as the career of a police officer is becoming less admirable and less remunerative.

Perhaps this dissonance has come about from the increasing liberal views of society and their demands for equal rights; or maybe the misconstrued opinions of the media are to blame. Regardless of who or what is seemingly culpable, this rising controversy continues to result in hostile consequences; and a civil war, amidst our nation, seems forthcoming unless the matter is resolved.

It is because of my deep concerns about these dire issues that I have enlarged the message of this novel. It bewilders me to view the negative amounts of news articles that feature stories involving police officer encounters. Stories about issues such as police officers on trial, cities protesting because the court ruled that an officer was justified in his actions, officers misusing their authority, or unlawful citizens threatening and assaulting the police are rapidly emerging on a daily basis. We stand gaping on the curbside, wondering what is true and what to do about it. Truly the air is prickling with a certain fate, and each of us must try to do something to preserve peace and security in the nation as we have known it...or we will lose it.

FERGUSON

In 2014, the city of Ferguson, a relatively small suburb in Missouri, would become nationally known within a day's notice. On August 9th, Officer Darren Wilson had a confrontation with 18-year-old, Michael Brown. Michael had carried out a robbery at a convenient store just minutes before, and the encounter resulted in the fatal shooting of the boy. Details about the story, true and false, went wild as the local community quickly learned of the news breaking event. With the assistance of the media, information about the incident expeditiously spread throughout the world that the boy was unarmed and black and that he was shot by a white officer. Discrimination disputes heaved forward and the community of Ferguson, as well as communities across the nation, became outraged. Unruly tensions erupted the following day and violent protests followed as citizens, within and around Ferguson, burned businesses, vandalized vehicles, threw rocks and Molotov cocktails, and looted stores that ensued abandonment due to the violence. Contentions continued for months, and the relationship between the public and law enforcement was severely impaired, not only within the community of Ferguson, but across the nation. Ultimately, in November that same year, the U.S. department of justice came to a conclusion about the case reporting that the witnesses corroborating with the officer's account were credible and were also supported by the forensic investigation; whereas, the incriminating witnesses were not credible, some of them finally admitting that they had not actually seen the event. Ultimately, the evidence concluded that officer Wilson shot Michael Brown in self-defense. The decision of the Grand Jury to not indict Officer Wilson led to further rioting and protests. This unfortunate incident demonstrated how quickly civil disorder could occur with controversial issues, and also exhibited the power that the media has on the public.

THE INFLUENCE OF THE MEDIA

The media is esteemed as an authority of opinion; and when *they* guide the public about their views, people believe them, whether it's true or not. Often the phrase "according to the media" is used when anyone of authority is revealing the source they heard the information from. Thus, we tend to assume the media is completely credible. Additionally, the media, utilizing internet, radio, television and other advanced technology, has access to delivering news globally and quickly. Within minutes of an incident, the entire world can be informed about a news breaking event.

Networks vary in their voice and opinions and strive to satisfy their audiences to keep their businesses alive. Deadlines must be met and reporters must be competitive to keep their jobs. In the process, stories can become misconstrued. As stories are released, radical groups may feed off the opinions of the media, stirring up disputations to achieve their personal interests. The combination can result in lethal consequences such as in the Ferguson ordeal. Not all police-related incidents stir up public reactions and lead to horrendous civil chaos, like Ferguson, yet the media has a vital stake in the perceptions of society. Other visual influences may also sway the beliefs of the public, such as those within the entertainment industry, which may be partly to blame for society's way of thinking.

THE INFLUENCE OF FILM AND TELEVISION

How we perceive things is highly due to the environment that surrounds us. Although we become educated through our own personal experiences, there are other ways that affect how we internalize concepts and ideals. We obtain information from books, teachers, nature, the internet, documentaries and many other available resources. We observe others to gain understanding. We ask questions and make choices, all to establish our own opinions and beliefs.

We also acquire knowledge through our senses. We remember sights, smells, sounds, tastes, and touches. One of the most persuasive senses is our vision. What we see, and the images we take in, powerfully affects our core beliefs. For instance, magicians perform impossible things and, although it isn't logical, we believe it because we see it. Since our visual sense is so influential, movies are often used for educational purposes as well as propaganda.

Through increased technology, images from the screen are powerfully driven by talented directors and actors of stories we are easily apt to embrace. Strangely, these movies have a way of influencing us to empathize with the beliefs of writers and producers of the films we view. It happens when we sit in front of a television or large movie screen, succumbing to the characters, usually the protagonist. We feel as though we are the main character and it is through our eyes that we watch the plot unfold, believing we are experiencing and feeling what the main character is. Seeing the film in 3D or 4D makes it even more convincing. We live the fantasy as we become actors of our own hearts. This makes us vulnerable to falsely altering our core inner beliefs, changing our previous opinions with virtual reality, and replacing with fiction our individual sense of life previously based on true facts or personal experiences.

Television and films have also increased in violence over the last decades. According to a study by the Parents Television Council, nearly half of the programs aired on five different networks, from January to February, contained violence. Nearly a third contained gun violence. We may become desensitized to this form of entertainment and believe that problems should be resolved with violent action, as we so diligently observe.

    As far as law enforcement is concerned, movies have had a huge impact on how the public has viewed public safety workers. Throughout the history of film, movies have fluctuated in how they depict police officers. Keystone Kops of the *silent film* days were illustrated as incompetent policemen, adding extra comedy to audiences who loved to laugh. *Slap stick* films, in the early 1900's, often portrayed the police as head-bopping, whistle-blowers who chased lovable characters, like Charlie Chaplin, with the intent of throwing him in jail. As film evolved, in the following years, police officers were depicted as heroic detectives and fearless agents in movies like the James Bond and Tom Cruise films, as well as villainous sheriffs and corrupt police officers in movies like *The Departed, Training Day* and *Bad Lieutenant*. It is easy to see how society could question whether police officers are heroes or villains.

AN ORDINARY HERO

Superheroes are adored for their miraculous attributes; they possess super powers and are admired for being extraordinary. Amidst the Spiderman senses, Batman powers, and Ironman invincibility and intelligence, how can a police officer compare when society's views of a hero are so fantastical.

It isn't surprising that a desensitized society, engrossed in the thrill of a *Marvel Comics* world influenced by the film industry, has nearly forgotten that ordinary law enforcement workers are literal heroes in every sense. They don't climb walls; they don't fly in cool cars, or wear oversized, protective robotic uniforms. But police officers do patrol streets 24 hours a day to assure communities are safe. They wipe tears from mothers whose babies die from SIDS. They comfort drivers who accidentally hit and kill pedestrians. They protect homes from burglaries and recover stolen properties. And a few of them take a bullet protecting us. Yet, they have become lost in the public's fictitious expectations of what a real hero is supposed to be.

REVERSING ROLES

It isn't enough that police officers must contend for the title of a hero. A new trend has emerged in film, afflicting law enforcement with an additional challenge concerning community acceptance. In the days of the *Lone Ranger* and *Zorro*, characters were loved for *conquering* evil. Today, characters are loved for *being* evil like Gollum in *The Lord of the Rings*, Darth Vader in *Star Wars*, Joker in *The Dark Knight*, Loki from *Thor*, and vampires and zombies in just about any film. Villains are admired for being cool, athletic, attractive, powerful, or funny. The trouble with loving villains comes when they are justified in their actions and law enforcement becomes the *bad guys* for locking them up. Years ago, little kids wanted to be the good guy who stopped bad guys from stealing and killing. Now, the roles seem reversed where being the bad guy is cool because he was played by an attractive and talented actor in a captivating film. It is stunning to witness the coming to pass of the prophetic warning given by the prophet Isaiah in the Bible: "Woe unto them that call evil good, and good evil".

DECEPTION

In some movies, the hero turns into the villain. Films with such examples are *The God Father* with Michael Corleone, *The Dark Knight* with Harvey Dent, and more recently and reaching more juvenile audiences, *Frozen* with Prince Hans. These fallen protagonists were credulously good in the beginning, then they betrayed us by adversely switching character. Thus, we are challenged to trust heroes because they are capable of turning evil.

Some films portray villains as protagonists who started bad then turned good, living happily ever after. Examples of these fantastical transformations are Gru from *Despicable Me*, Grinch from *How the Grinch Stole Christmas*, Megamind from *Megamind*, Dr. Otto Octavius from *Spiderman 2* and Severus Snape from *Harry Potter*. These movies glamorize villains as really heroes in disguise, having good deep within them, waiting for someone to come along to aid in their retransformation. Having hope in mankind and their ability to change is one thing, but communities should use caution when trusting that criminals will turn their lives around, as depicted in such movies. Although there have been a handful of successes with convicts re-entering back into society, according to a study by the Bureau of Justice Statistics in April of 2014, recidivism, or the tendency to relapse into criminal behavior, was extremely high. The study consisted of tracking 405,000 criminals from about 30 different U.S. states, for five years following their release from prison, to see where they would end up. Before the end of three years, approximately 68 percent were arrested for a new crime; with more than half being arrested before the end of the first year, and about 37 percent returning to prison within 6 months following their release. By the end of five years, 77 percent had been arrested again. Recidivism varied in percentages, according to the type of crimes and the attributes of the inmates. Inmates arrested for crimes involving violence, drugs, or property offenses were more likely to be incarcerated again for the same crime. Sympathizing with hard-core criminals might result in allowing them more mercy and less penalties, which could have catastrophic consequences in the end. If the most heavily guarded prisons could speak, they might attest that many of the criminals they hold are extremely dangerous and far from having any glimmer of good left within them. One officer of a prison, that our local religious youth group visited one year, refused to even allow us to walk through the same building that the hard core prisoners were housed in, due to the perilous risk it posed. The officer explained that the prisoners in that facility were so dark, being captive to a tenaciously evil will, that they seemed as though they no longer had a conscience. Hope for any of them returning to lives of goodness was doused in their constant desire to threaten and kill the guards anytime one of them would come near them. Though many prisoners could benefit from programs improving their lives and integrating them back into society, it seems riskier to invest in prisoners who would pose danger to the public by being allowed back into communities.

REWRITTEN AND TWISTED

Liberal views may have helped to shape some movie productions where the stories were rewritten to turn the original antagonist into the protagonist such as Maleficient, who was the evil villain in *Sleeping Beauty* but the mistreated and misunderstood victim in *Maleficient*. In the *Wizard of Oz*, the Wicked Witch of the West is obviously evil; whereas, *Wicked*, portrays the Wicked Witch of the West as the victim of ill circumstances. Twisting the character roles of villains in these contemporary films challenges the standards and morals of the older generations about stories that have been told for decades.

CRIME JUSTIFIED

In the 2013 American film, *Now You See Me*, villains become justified in their actions, and forgiven for their crimes. Using the delight of illusionists, mentalists, escapists, hypnotists and psychics, the movie wittily charms us with magic tricks that create heroes out of criminal magicians. We are entranced to believe that two wrongs make a right as the magicians vindictively give money they steal to people who are victims of hard times. People are framed to satisfy a lingering debt of revenge, and the entire crime is condoned. The female Interpol agent even falls for the mastermind villain, as she betrays justice for her heart. Overall, viewers are persuaded to side with the criminals because their actions are enticing and rectifying.

ANCIENT CRIME

Since the beginning of mankind, the establishment of laws was crucial for maintaining security, peace and order. One of the earliest documented accounts of crime between two people comes from the bible, in the book of Genesis, where Cain killed Abel. A law had been established by God, but the law was broken and the violation occurred. Laws continued to be broken throughout the progression of history, and law enforcement organizations were established as populations increased.

Throughout the centuries, civilizations around the world have established law-enforcing organizations comprising of brotherhoods, militias, posses and police forces. Peace keepers have been known as watchmen, guards, prefects, vigiles, peelers, Bobbies, constables, inspectors, detectives, sheriffs, troopers, rangers, and police officers. Their duties have consisted of apprehending thieves, keeping order, maintaining crowd control during big events, arresting lawbreakers, preventing crimes, and protecting the people.

As benevolent as its design was, law enforcement wasn't exactly efficient, and crime continued to increase with each growing decade. In the early 1800's, many towns in England took initiative to improve their police agencies. Laws passed allowing funding to occur, and advanced uniformed police forces to emerge. A short time later, the United States patterned their police forces after those in England. Ultimately, stronger and more centralized organizations evolved, enabling the formation of the crime prevention and crime solving institutions that we benefit from today.

A HOUSE DIVIDED

Despite the advancement of law enforcement, criminal activity has far from dissolved. Crime rates continue to rise as populations increase, and police agencies battle to keep up with the increasing demands to protect the citizens within their jurisdiction. Additionally, the strain on peaceful communities has heightened with public disputes against the law, especially when a criminal is shot and killed by a police officer. Although it is healthy for people to question their governing leaders and challenge a system to keep it in check, it is harmful for people to create a civil war among themselves. Resolving issues with the law should be negotiated under harmonious circumstances. Nations in the past have self-destructed or resulted in horrific battle due to internal conflict when matters were dealt with maliciously and violently. In 1858, Abraham Lincoln delivered a speech declaring, "A house divided against itself cannot stand," warning the nation of the peril that was at hand concerning the United States. America engaged in the Civil War only a few short years later. But Lincoln's exhortation was influenced by the counsel of an even greater role leader. In Matthew 12:25, Jesus warned: E*very kingdom divided against itself is brought to desolation; and every city or house divided against itself shall not stand.* Truly, the consequences of Jesus' prophetic warning rang true throughout history. From the ancient civil wars of the Roman Empire and the crusader Kingdom of Jerusalem, to the modern, on-going conflicts of Afghanistan and Syria, nations have been brought to ruins. But is it possible to avoid internal conflict within nations when people are so diverse that disagreements are inevitable? Can agreements be so contentious that they cannot be resolved by any other way except by war?

RESOLUTIONS

Certainly, we are surrounded by deteriorating morals in an imperfect world. Most values seem to be dissolving, due to the uprising liberal views of people who obsessively challenge the current system and want to modernize, or people who constantly instigate hostile debates concerning controversial topics. Extremists, civil rights activists and sectarians are taking part in the pandemonium for their own objectives, and criminals are taking advantage of the rising disorder as America cascades down the slope of growing rebellion and chaos. Additionally, we have high expectations for keeping peace and order, yet low tolerance for the mistakes of those required to maintain security in our communities. When the law occasionally fails, we quickly lose trust in the entire public safety system. It is true, that there has been good reason to be concerned when error occurs within Law Enforcement. Cases where innocent citizens were mistakenly arrested for crimes they didn't commit, or incidents where police officers were discovered to be corrupt or injurious to citizens, brings distrust to a service we depend so heavily upon. Communities keeping the system in check will help to purge police departments of dishonest workers and prevent an abundance of unfortunate errors upon innocent people. But when societal scrutiny pushes too far, debilitating the police forces, adverse effects may result. How do we balance a productive level of surveillance; and how can we refrain from eradicating the whole law enforcement program when someone blunders?

To resolve conflicts, both parties of opposing opinions would obviously need to negotiate their views and work out a concordant solution. Unfortunately, when both sides are equally unrelenting, the friction erupts into a blazing battle. If the right conditions exist, the fury will escalate to internal war resulting in violence and bloodshed. Perhaps a lack of education may have something to do with the problem.

Many police departments, who are seeking to bridge the gap between law enforcement workers and the citizens they serve, are developing educational programs to unite communities. By educating the citizens about their procedures, many misunderstandings might be avoided and disputes dissolved. In fall of 2015, the Bountiful, Utah Police Department held a training event to demonstrate the pressures that officers go through during "high risk" traffic calls. With the number of officer-involved shootings escalating over the last few years, it has become more important for citizens to understand why certain tactics are being used and what dangers police officers face in order to keep families and communities safe. The Bountiful Police Department believes that a good relationship between the community and police is essential in strengthening the partnership between them.

A WORLD WITHOUT LAW ENFORCEMENT

Communities continue to expand in population and controversial ideas. As movies and books are created from the imaginations of writers depicting a utopia gone wrong, reflecting the increase of evil in the world today, we are led to contemplate the outcome, good or bad. Regardless of our circumstances, our fate depends on our choices. We can choose to become informed of the issues at hand, and make an effort to become involved in the good of society, or we can blame others and do nothing but watch the world slip into a fiery pit of calamity.

As many apocalyptic movies depict, the government system and law enforcement is overthrown by rebels and the law is taken into the hands of the people. Movies don't show the truth of such scenarios amidst indestructible heroic characters who can't be killed because it would ruin the story plot. Truly, a civil world, with a just law enforcement, is worth preserving.

Nevertheless, many citizens rally for the civil rights of criminals. Lawsuits against the police have increased and riots have intensified. Despite the multiple stories informing people of police-involved shootings, the public is scarcely informed of the innumerous times where officers have held fire and displayed restraint amidst extreme situations, often receiving injury from the assailants. Additionally, police officers work under insanely dangerous circumstances, yet are practically expected to spin gold out of straw. Studies have shown that even well-trained officers are unable to demonstrate consistency to fire their weapon in time as a suspect raises their gun and fires first. Split-second decisions become exceedingly difficult even during the most ideal situations. In 2013, all in the line of duty, twenty-seven police officers were murdered and nearly 50,000 were assaulted.

Yet, society still sways to the sympathies of unlawful citizens claiming injustice. Frustration between the law and the public is evident, but setting aside the apocalyptic movies, imagine what the nation would really be like if there were no lawful boundaries and there were no police officers to prevent crime and ensure personal safety.

As it is, people try to get away with crime when the law does exist. But many are not so eager, knowing there are consequences. Take away the law, and you take away the punishment. Not only would crime that already occurs with the law in place go unpunished, but the crime index would explode. Looters, at will, would break the glass of windows of businesses. Thieves would openly steal from the shelves of stores and not be stopped. People would solve their own disputes using knives, guns, or whatever they could get their hands on. Banks would be robbed and houses would be broken into. Murders would increase and the economy would plummet. Without law enforcement, our stable and secure society would quickly crumble. Drug abuse, rape, arson, assault, battery and vehicular-related crimes would overtake neighborhood streets, eradicating security and the quality of living. Life would consist strictly on how to survive, and progression would dissolve.

A crime report for Chicago revealed that over 150,000 crimes took place in 2010. Among those crimes, more than 400 were murders, over 1,400 were criminal sexual assaults, over 14,000 were robberies and approximately 19,000 were motor vehicle thefts. Gun related crimes reached 4,000, with aggravated assault or battery reaching a total of 14,000 cases. Arson hit 500, and theft was over 75,000. Other categorized assaults and robberies totaled an unfathomable figure for one year of crimes reflecting in only one city.

Chicago does have one of the highest crime indexes in the nation, but all other states have equally astonishing crime reports. In Utah, the crime rate that occurred in a 24 hour period in 2012 was 246 crimes. These were crimes that occurred with a law enforcement system in place. Police officers responded to each of these crimes, restoring order and justice to cities that were violated. Consequences were issued to offenders, discouraging others from wanting to follow suit.

Law enforcement workers make a difference in the world. Without them, our standard of living would truly descend. To preserve the safety and rights of citizens, the law must be preserved and the public must take a logical look at the alternative consequences if the law were to be dismantled. Restoring respect and trust to the law enforcement system might require the cooperation of communities to join together with police departments to unite society with a system that works together for the same objective: peace and security. Investing in programs that educate the vast and diverse population of the United States concerning the duties of a police officer might be a good place to begin.

THE MESSAGE OF THE GLOCK

The Glock, or any gun for that matter, often represents the power to defend. If used appropriately, the device can protect and represent security. If misused, the weapon can destroy lives, physically and emotionally, and become a symbol of violence. I designed the cover for *The Other Side of a Glock* and asked my talented daughter, Rachel Allred, to create it. Two pistols facing each other represent the contentions exploding between the society and law enforcement over the power to defend. It was my hope for readers to see a better perspective of both sides when it came to the conflict between communities and the law, and gain a better understanding, leading to a determination to resolve disagreements peacefully. I also wanted to give a visual of how police officers may feel when they are facing criminals with or without weapons. It takes a lot of courage to be on the other side of a Glock with the lives of the entire community on your shoulders.

CHAPTER 1

FACING DEATH

MORE THAN ORDINARY

It was a cold but average morning on January 18, 2002 when Jim awoke to the stillness of the dark. It was 6 a.m. and the nip in the outside air, made it more inviting to remain under the warm covers, but Jim forced himself out of bed.

Mornings for Jim were far from routine. When he enlisted as a police officer, he knew that schedules would fluctuate. He took turns with the other officers in the department covering all 24 hours, seven days a week with varying shifts. Day shift began at 7 a.m. and ended at 5 p.m. Swing overlapped the day workers, beginning at 3pm and ending at 1am. Grave yard was from 9 p.m. to 7 a.m. It was Jim's turn to work day shift.

Quietly, Jim dressed in his uniform, using the dim light

coming from the bathroom. He pulled on his pants and shirt, trying not to disturb Melanie. Certainly there should be some sort of reality show on dressing without waking your spouse. He buckled his belt and then glanced towards the bed where his sweetheart lay comfortably under the blankets. If she stirred or appeared to be awake, he would lean over and give her a kiss goodbye. That morning merited a kiss but Melanie would barely remember it.

From the bedroom, Jim strolled through the hallway, passing one of the children's rooms before entering the kitchen to find his police jacket. Usually he wasn't hungry that early, so breakfast would come later when he would pick up something on the road. Jim reached for his jacket, hanging on the back of a kitchen chair, where he left it the night before. He slipped it on, welcoming some protection from the cold winter world he was about to enter.

The kitchen counters were randomly scattered with papers from his children. A math assignment or English paper from the twins, and artwork from his eight-year-old son, Casey. A cup or two was sitting near the sink, but there was no evidence of the dinner from the night before, as Melanie had washed the dishes and wiped off the table. Contentedly, Jim smiled before zipping up his coat and heading for the door.

Stepping out into the chilly darkness, he breathed in deeply, acclimating to the sudden temperature change. He turned to lock the front door then stepped towards his patrol car where he climbed inside, strapped on his seatbelt, and then started the engine. Nothing seemed to indicate that this day would be different than any other day.

Jim slowly pulled out of the driveway and started towards the Orem City Police Department Building. Passing houses down his street, a light would occasionally appear in a window, and then another as the city slowly awoke with the morning sunrise. Soon the house lights became less noticeable as the first soft glow of the sun transformed the dark musty sky. Gradually the atmosphere lit up to a hazy gray. On spring and summer days, the sky would have warmed with coral hues, but January's inversion fought against nature's majestic artistry, resulting in a dull and polluted canvas that was overwhelmed by drab skies.

It was only about 15 minutes to the office, but sitting in a quiet car seemed much longer when self conversations ran out of things to say. Jim pulled into the familiar parking lot of the Orem

Police Department then entered the building.

Sergeant Ron Carlson was already in his office finishing up paperwork from the day before. "Mornin', Flygare," he called from his desk.

"Good Morning, Sergeant." Jim was more reserved than most, and he wasn't in for conversation that early, so he continued past the sergeant to check in for the day.

After briefing with the officer from the shift before, Jim took to the streets, patrolling the city of Orem. It was almost nine o'clock and his stomach began to growl reminding him that it was time for breakfast. He picked up a doughnut and soda at the nearest convenient store and climbed back into his car. The sugar coated bread tasted especially good first thing in the morning. After a couple of bites, the dispatcher called into his radio. "348, a 10-47 in progress,"

"348, go ahead," Jim responded into his radio.

"800 North and Main, apartment complex, suspicion of auto burglary in progress."

"348, copy," Jim replied. He placed his half-eaten pastry on the passenger seat and quickly started the car.

As he headed towards 800 North and Main, Jim's mind went to work, running through different scenarios about the confrontation he might have. With a burglar right in the middle of committing an auto theft, there was a great chance that the perpetrator would try to flee once he saw the police car, so Jim geared up for a chase. Usually the chase would be vehicular, unless the guy was caught in the garage. Then the scene might include a firm persuasion for the thief to give himself up. As he thought about several recourses, he casually reached for the rest of his doughnut and decided that the call sounded low key. He even anticipated that he might arrive at the scene and discover that the burglar had already taken off. This meant he would have to search for possible witnesses and interview them to find out if they had seen anything. Jim frowned, imagining the long drawn-out reports that lie ahead if that were the case.

As Jim neared the apartment complex, he acknowledged to the dispatcher that he had arrived on scene. He spoke with composed clarity. There wasn't anything in this situation that should cause him to be afraid; besides, the dispatcher had not indicated that there were any threats or weapons. Even if the situation proved daunting, Jim wouldn't let fear consume him.

As a police officer, every day posed numerous possibilities for fear. Traffic stops meant confrontations with strangers. Calls which varied with disputes, car accidents, aggravated assaults, weapon confrontations, and suicides were all frightening. But there wasn't time to entertain fear because, on many occasions, Jim had to act fast which meant he had to think fast. Jim didn't discount fear. It was a natural built-in warning system, alerting him of potential dangers. It kept him from doing stupid things that might result in injury or death, and it aided in human survival. Its purpose was to promote the production of necessary chemicals, to give energy and strength when dangerous situations did arise. It took the form of discomfort, like when he was interviewed for the Orem Police Department for a position on their team. It caused him to push a little harder and be a little better to achieve what he hoped for.

Fear also had adverse effects. It created worry, like the time when Jim first asked Melanie on a date and he worried about being rejected. Fear was also deceiving. It could make you think it had your best interest in mind, and then disable you. It clouded reason and created consternation at critical times. Jim had seen people paralyzed by fear; and they suffered terrible consequences as a result. Thinking ahead was the key. Formulating in your mind, in advance, how you were going to handle a situation. It gave you the upper hand over fear. Leaving actions to chance, when emotions were surmounting, led to disaster at any level. Jim didn't like those odds. He wanted to be ready to respond well to any ordeal, to protect the city of Orem and maintain peace. They counted on him, and it was in his nature to fulfill every measure of a police officer.

As Jim arrived at the apartment complex, he slowly pulled into the parking lot and scanned the property. Next to the apartments in question, a man was standing outside of a red pickup truck that harbored a washing machine in the bed. He was probably a maintenance guy, or even a neighbor. Jim sighed as he prepared to interview the man, thinking of the paperwork this call would produce.

Jim got out of his car. The man saw Jim and got into the red truck. Jim raised his brow as he watched the man drive about 50 yards to another part of the complex.

Maybe he didn't realize I wanted to speak with him, Jim rationalized to himself as he returned to his patrol car. He drove towards the red truck, as the man was getting out again. By this time, Sergeant Carlson, who was Jim's backup, had arrived and pulled up to Jim's car.

Jim got out of his car the second time and proceeded towards the man, feeling more cautious then he had before. Suddenly the guy gave a look of terror and bolted, jumping back into the red truck and speeding off. As Jim ran back towards his patrol car, he quickly concluded that this man was the suspect in question. Sergeant Carlson took off after the truck, and Jim followed the sergeant.

The burglar drove recklessly through the parking lot, tearing across residential lawns and wrecking property. He circled around the complex, turned right onto 800 North, and then made another sharp right onto the street dividing the apartment buildings. Sergeant Carlson, followed closely behind, tightly making every turn and swerving to miss the stolen washing machine as it toppled out of the back of the red truck.

Jim was right behind the chase; but when the assailant and Sergeant turned right, Jim continued on straight to the next road. He turned right on 100 West and drove parallel to the vehicular pursuit, hoping to cut the burglar off at the top of the street. Jim floored his car, passing the sergeant and the red truck and then made a sharp right, now driving towards the chase.

Seeing Jim approach, the thief abruptly stopped his truck and tore out of the vehicle. Jim remained in his patrol car and continued to follow the man who was now fleeing on foot. Jim didn't know that the thief was carrying a stolen 9mm hand gun that had been taken in a burglary months before. Jim was also unaware that the man was Ricardo Griaz, a criminal possessing a lengthy history of arrests throughout Utah County including vehicle burglary, theft, and assorted drug charges. Ricardo had become more dangerous with each new offense stemming back from 1996. Just prior to stealing the red pickup truck that day, Ricardo had vowed to his friends that he would not allow himself to be arrested by the police, no matter what the cost.

Sergeant Carlson had stopped his car behind the truck and jumped out to follow Ricardo to chase the assailant on foot. As Ricardo ran around one of the apartment buildings, Jim drove over the curb and onto the grass alongside of Ricardo. Somehow Jim's lights and sirens turned on by themselves. Jim was surprised by this, because he hadn't touched the controls. Nevertheless, he remained focused on the suspect.

Ricardo went through a gate. *He's trapped*, Jim thought, believing the fence was part of a complete enclosure. This would box him in and cause him to surrender. Jim soon discovered, with great disappointment, that the yard was not fully fenced and Ricardo escaped, disappearing past the adjoining building. Jim stopped his car on the grass and tore out after Ricardo, leaving the sirens blaring and the lights flashing. Slipping past the partial enclosure and around the building, he spotted Ricardo. Ricardo ran towards 800 North, taking Jim back to the original route he had led when the pursuit first began.

Meanwhile, Sergeant Carlson had lost sight of Ricardo and was determining which way to go through the maze of apartments. He heard the blaring of Jim's Siren's and ran towards the direction of the patrol car, not knowing that Ricardo had circled around again. If the Sergeant had turned the other way, he would have eventually found himself dangerously face to face with the burglar.

Ricardo continued to flee with great speed, but Jim was in excellent shape and caught up quickly. "Stop and put your hands up! I'm a police officer!" Jim yelled out several times. As he got closer, his mind was turning. He thought: *I've got to decide what I'm going to do once I reach him.* Jim recalled his training and his pre-contemplation about a situation like this and he quickly decided that he would take the man down in one shot, without wrestling him. By this time, he was practically running on Ricardo's heels. Jim threw his leg out to trip Ricardo, and the burglar went down. Ricardo quickly rolled over and knelt up with his back to Jim.

Stopping abruptly and breathing hard, Jim stared back at Ricardo, less than five feet away. Suddenly, from the corner of his left eye, Jim saw a black object appear over Ricardo's shoulder. Jim thought: *Is that a gun?* He hadn't expected that. He had been running full speed behind Ricardo and hadn't seen him pull out the handgun from his belt.

Jim started to back off when Ricardo fired over his shoulder, his back still turned to the officer.

Jim instinctively pulled his gun and shot back, engaging with Ricardo. All at once, it was as if he was on autopilot. He was in a reactive state, acting with the mind-set he had previously instilled within his subconscious during his training at the police academy. Bullets flew past him yet Jim stayed focused, even though all of his training at the academy could not have prepared him for what was happening.

A bullet tore through Jim's police jacket, and he felt something hit his arm, but he continued shooting until Ricardo finally stopped, dropping his gun in front of him. Ricardo collapsed but then attempted to grab his gun again. Jim quickly stepped towards the gun and kicked the semi-automatic pistol out of reach. Ricardo gasped and fell unconscious.

The threat was over and the shooting had ceased but the sound of gunfire continued to ring loudly in Jim's head. With his gun still aimed at Ricardo, Jim couldn't move. He was frozen in place, staring back at a man lying lifelessly on the ground. A man he had shot in self defense.

Jim was trained to protect. Not only had Jim saved his own life, but he had stopped a dangerous criminal who was whirling down a raging river of crime that swept up countless victims. This man defied the law and challenged the system by insisting he would not be arrested by the police. He selfishly filled his hunger for money and drugs at the expense of innocent people by stealing from them. With a gun in his possession, it wouldn't be long before someone else's life might be taken. Jim knew he did what had to be done.

Sergeant Carlson finally caught up to the scene and quickly assessed what had happened. Later, he would share with Jim, his startling observation: that if he had gone the other way, instead of towards Jim's patrol car, he would have met the thief head on and he might not have been as quick to draw his gun. The outcome certainly would have been different.

Sergeant approached Jim, who still had his gun pointed at Ricardo. Jim was too stunned to realize he was in shock. He thought he was fine, yet somehow he couldn't remember how to put his gun back in his holster.

"Replace your gun, Flygare," the sergeant instructed, gingerly stepping towards him.

Jim heard him, but he couldn't process it.

The sergeant repeated himself, but Jim still didn't move. Sergeant immediately perceived that Jim was traumatized and needed detailed instructions. "Okay, Jim, you're gonna bend your arm and move it backwards," he elaborated. "That's good, now slide your gun back in the holster...your holster is hooked to your belt. That's right." He then led Jim to the other side of the road and tried to get him to sit down on the curb, but Jim refused, too dazed to notice the sergeant calling for medical help. His hearing had quieted, and he felt like there was no one else around. He hadn't heard the chorus of sirens, or seen additional officers come as emergency vehicles pulled up. Then, suddenly, they were all there, like they appeared out of nowhere. Jim was even numb to the pain in his arm where he had been shot.

One of the arriving officers attempted to get Jim to sit down in one of the police cars, but he wouldn't. Another sergeant joined in trying to persuade Jim that he needed to sit down and relax. "Come on, Jim. You need to take it easy."

"I'm fine," Jim protested.

"We need to take your jacket off and take a look at your arm," a medic gently instructed.

Jim shook his head, glancing down at his arm assuming blood would spill out from the wound. He knew he'd been shot, but he feared what he'd see if his jacket was removed. Perhaps his arm was half missing. It seemed reasonable to keep it on until...until things returned to normal again.

It took some negotiating, but the medics and officers finally got Jim to take his jacket off. They discovered Jim had been hit by muzzle blast, revealing how close he had actually been standing to Ricardo when the guns were engaging. Fortunately, the bullet had only grazed him, wounding the top layers of his skin. It was a miracle Jim wasn't killed.

They put Jim in an ambulance, but he still believed he was fine. He felt normal, even though his heart was racing at a dangerous level. Sergeant Carlson watched the emergency vehicle drive away as snow began to fall.

In the ambulance, one of the medics struggled to place an oxygen mask on Jim. He recognized the medic; he had trained at the police academy with him. "Thanks, but I don't need it." Jim took it off.

"Yes you do, Jim," the medic insisted. "It's to help you. Oxygen is like medication." He placed the mask back on him.

Jim felt like he couldn't breathe with the mask covering his face so he yanked it back off, wondering why the medic was talking to him like he was an irrational child. It was a continuous battle, all the way to the hospital and Jim couldn't understand why they wanted him to have it.

At the hospital, they dressed Jim's wound, but Jim still refuse to wear the oxygen mask. Finally, the doctor came into the room. "Jim, your heart rate is so high right now that we are going to have to medicate you."

"No, I don't want to be medicated," Jim became more irritated. "I told you, I'm fine! I feel good enough to go home!"

"You don't understand," the doctor said, sternly. "If we let you continue with a heart rate as high as yours, you won't live long enough to go home. You need to start calming down now and cooperate which means you need to wear the oxygen to see if we can get your heart rate down that way. Otherwise we'll have to medicate you and admit you for a couple of days."

Jim didn't like the idea of staying at the hospital so he finally consented. He didn't realize that when people go into shock as extreme as he did, they are not aware of what is really happening to their body. The body is in overdrive, and it could self destruct.

After some time, Jim's heart rate dropped to a safe enough level, that they released him from the hospital that afternoon. He later learned that Ricardo had died that same day. Although, Jim was a hero, he felt forlorn. A life was taken and it stung, no matter how terrible the criminal was.

ANOTHER WITNESS

Jim took administrative leave for the investigation of the incident and his arm healed up just fine. But he was rattled and relived the shooting in continuous nightmares. Also, Jim was bothered about not seeing Ricardo pull out his gun. He had run over and over the scene in his mind but couldn't figure out how he had missed such a key clue. Jim beat himself up over it.

Not long after the shooting, Jim bumped into a past friend from high school. As they were talking, the friend revealed to Jim that on the day of the shooting he happened to be driving down the road where it all occurred; going the opposite way that Jim was running as he chased the thief. "Do you realize I was right there and I saw everything leading up to the whole gun fight?" his friend asked. "I saw the guy running down the road. As he was running, he pulled the gun out from his belt and racked it. I saw what was going to happen but couldn't do anything about it because I was in my car going the other direction and they wouldn't let anyone near the scene once I got turned around."

The news was relieving to Jim. He hadn't been negligent after all. He realized he never could have seen Ricardo pull the gun, not the way it was taking place. Jim was grateful for his friend's strange coincidence that brought him consolation.

MAKING A DIFFERENCE

Several years after the shooting, and a year before he retired, Jim responded to a call at a house concerning a neighborhood complaint. After going to the door and talking with the man at the house for a while, the man started telling how a few years earlier his red pickup truck was stolen and then returned. Jim realized that it was the same truck that was stolen by Ricardo. The real owner of the red truck would never know that Jim was the one who recovered his vehicle and stopped the thief; and Jim modestly didn't tell him. But he realized the unseen impact that his efforts really made.

CHAPTER 2

THE POWER OF A MIND SET

At times, Jim reflected on his dangerous confrontation with Ricardo. Not every officer would encounter such a traumatic event in their entire life time. And those who did often experienced severe repercussions, resulting in psychological disorders or early retirement. Jim thought of the bullets as they flew past him, marveling how his mind could be totally engaged on one thing, yet allow for everything else around him to become seemingly invisible. He remembered how his focus had been exceedingly streamlined as he flipped into a survival or responsibility mode; it happened instantaneously. Before he knew it, he was completely engaged in the action at hand, and the underlying motivation was: *I've got to keep myself alive. I've got a responsibility to protect others from this guy.*

Jim had already told himself, ahead of time, how he would respond to an incident where someone pulled a gun out of nowhere and started to fire; and so he was able to perform the way he envisioned when the time called for it. Afterwards, when it was over, his defense mode shut down, as it was no longer needed, and all his other senses and natural emotions started to take over. That's when shock took the wheel and his heart rate skyrocketed. The emotional aftermath was one thing he hadn't prepared his mind for, because he had never experienced something like that before.

It wasn't until further on in his career that Jim realized that the mind-set survival technique he had created and utilized was a life-saving strategy he had unknowingly developed. He would later teach this technique to other officers as a firearms instructor.

TEACHING

Jim was a firearms instructor for a short time before he retired. One thing he would teach his students was how they had to develop a mind set. The mind is reactive. There were times when you had to react to an incident and you didn't have time to think about it. With the shooting, he remembered it being like a relentlessly fast cycle. He could see what was going on, and then his body responded according to how he had programmed it to do when creating his mind set. It was a hundred percent reactive. In the middle of the shooting, he didn't stop and say, "Hmm. Someone is shooting at me. Which reaction should I choose?" There was no thinking involved, because there wasn't time. And so his subconscious thinking determined his next move, not his conscious thinking. It was crucial that your mind-set was thorough and that you could follow through using your subconscious programming.

He'd often imagine various situations that he might possibly get a call about, and then he would formulate in his head what he would try and do if he had to deal with that specific ordeal. He thought of many different scenarios, and would avoid dwelling on the peril of any given circumstance, but he'd think out beforehand what would be the best way to quickly react. This strategy improved his ability to make quick decisions and to respond to incidents with focus and rational thinking. Jim didn't feel nervous or afraid before the calls he'd respond to, because he already knew ahead of time, with his mind-set technique, of what he had to do to protect himself and those around him. Sometimes he would get scared after the incident, once he realized the danger of it all, but prior to and during the incident, he was confident because of his mind set.

    Jim continued to practice his mind-set exercises throughout his career, adding one more detail: dealing with shock afterward.

CHAPTER 3

RESPONDING TO CASES WITH CHILDREN

Often officers, like any normal human beings, are powerfully affected by disconcerting incidents they encounter. Especially those involving children. Children can be innocent victims in a society full of disadvantage and hazard. Their fate can occasionally be at the mercy of unrelenting mistakes that are bound to occur in an imperfect world. Regardless of how difficult or how traumatic, the job still calls for an officer to have strength and composure.

A LATE NIGHT WALK

When Jim was first starting out in the police force, he took a job at the prison and also a part time job as a reserve officer. Reserve officers were volunteers who did everything that full time officers did; they just didn't get paid. The advantage of working as a reserve officer was that it was a stepping stone to getting a full time job with the department when a position opened up. This way, the department could evaluate the reserve officers and hire someone who had already been working for them; someone who they had seen and known whether or not they were qualified for the position.

As a reserve officer, Jim would go on calls with one of his friends who worked as a full time police officer. One time, they received a phone call around one in the morning to investigate an accident. Jim went with his friend to respond to the scene on State Street in Lehi. A man had been driving his truck down a dark, unlit road and unknowingly passed two kids taking a late-night walk along the side of the street. As the truck passed the teens, the mirror fatally hit one of the boys, throwing him onto the grassy area near the road.

When Jim arrived to the scene, he saw the young teen-ager dead on the grass, and instantly became weak in the knees. This was his first encounter with a fatality.

They called out forensic nurses, who came to draw blood on the victim as well as on the truck driver. It was dark and the nurse, who was assigned to work on the boy, had Jim hold a flashlight on the victim's body so she could see what she was doing. The nurse pulled out a long, foot-length, needle that could reach into the heart to withdraw blood samples that would be used later by criminal investigators for examination. Jim watched the needle go into the boy in the spot of the flashlight, and he soon became woozy. Fearing that he might pass out, he knelt down, still obediently holding the light for the nurse. But watching the blood slowly seep into the collection tube wasn't the worst part for Jim. Going to the parents' house at two o'clock in the morning to give a death notice was more dreadful.

Jim and his partner were told of the boy's religion and located the congregational leader of his church, a bishop of the Church of Jesus Christ of Latter Day Saints. The officers asked the bishop to accompany them as they broke the news to the boy's parents and the bishop compassionately complied. When they all arrived at the house, every window was completely dark. Jim's knees suddenly felt weak again as he approached the front door. His knuckles knocking on the wood seemed to echo, piercing the silent, estranging night.

Soon, a light turned on in the bedroom, and then another one in the living room. Finally the outside light came on; shining upon the two officers and the bishop as though they were center stage and it was time to give their lines. The door opened and Jim spoke. "Sir, we're from the Lehi Police Department. May we come in?" A man squinted back at them; his eyes still not completely adjusted after having been in a deep sleep. He opened the door further, revealing his wife, curiously peering at the new visitors and holding her night robe closely around her body. Jim and his informative crew were invited in and the parents trembled, knowing that two officers and a bishop, standing in the living room at such an unprecedented time, dictated trouble.

Jim knew there was no easy way to break the news, so he determined to be point blank. "There's been an accident and your son was killed," he announced.

The dad buckled forward and the mother collapsed straight to the floor. It took a few minutes for the parents to recover and gain enough composure to hear the details of the accident and what needed to happen next.

After things were somewhat settled, the officers and the bishop left the house that had once been naively tranquil and was now emanating with anguish. Jim's heart seemed to grow heavier as he walked further away from the home. He had completed his assignment, but he couldn't forget the limp and lifeless boy and the lamenting parents. He felt strangely initiated into the police department.

For the next week, Jim was dazed. The incident seemed to provide him a reality check about life and death, and the impact was forever changing. As Jim worked that week at the prison, he talked with fellow workers about the fatality and it helped immensely. Talking about things always seemed to help. Often Jim would talk to other officers when he witnessed some pretty tough scenes. He learned, early on, that he had to be careful with whom he shared his information. People in law enforcement understood it because they experienced it. But most people outside of their realm couldn't relate with what an officer would go through and what traumatic things he would see. Jim couldn't just tell anything to anyone or it might be misconstrued or used against him or not necessarily appreciated. It was tricky to find the right person to vent to.

Not long after, Jim became a full time officer in Lehi, equipped with unforgettable insight and a presage of things to come.

COINS AND A BUS

An excited, five-year old boy sat next to his mother and sibling on a UTA bus, clutching a handful of coins feeling very *grown up*. His intentions were to spend his money at Kohlers, a grocery store in Lehi. He had visited the store many times before, and he could hardly contain himself. He eagerly watched through the bus windows for the Kohlers' sign to appear, which it finally did, and the bus came to its regular stop across the street from the store. Anxious to spend his coins, the little boy dashed ahead of his mother down the aisle towards the exit of the bus. The mother grabbed her other child, a younger sibling of the boy, and quickly followed behind her son. As soon as the boy got to the bottom of the bus steps and spotted Kohler's across the two-lane, two-way street on Main, he dashed across the road in front of the bus. He never saw the pickup truck, in the next lane, driven by a sixteen year old girl.

Jim was fairly new to his career when he received the call to the accident on Main Street. He had only been with the Lehi Police Department for less than a year. Jim arrived on scene and got out of his car. The first thing he noticed was coins scattered around the body of a lifeless little boy, lying in a pool of blood. He would learn later that the boy died instantly. Jim's heart sank, thinking of his own little son, but he mustered up courage. He had to. He was the only officer patrolling at that time. And there he was amidst a devastated 16-year old driver, a traumatized bus driver who witnessed everything front and center, and a mother who was completely in shock. Luckily the ambulance wasn't too far away, which would give Jim assistance and medical help.

Once the ambulance arrived and began working with the deceased boy and his mother, Jim approached the 16 year old girl to calm her and fill out a report. Struggling to feel adequate due to his lack of experience, he spoke softly to the girl, attempting to help settle her down as she trembled. Shortly after, Jim made his way towards the bus driver. Jim listened to the man as he emotionally recalled the images he had seen. It happened so fast. The pick-up truck had come from the lane next to the driver's side of the bus, going the same direction. The little boy ran out from the front of the bus then *smack*! It was a blind hit. And there wasn't time for the truck to stop, let alone time to yell any warnings. "Talking helps." Jim began. "When you go home tonight, keep talking about it with people you can trust, who will listen to you," Jim attempted to console but felt a little shaky, himself. "It's important not to keep your feelings inside. Let your friends and family help you. Can you do that?" The bus driver nodded. Jim knew he couldn't change what had just happened, but he was there at a critical moment, directing, instructing, and comforting.

PLAYING WITH GUNS

Jim was working a day shift as a police officer in Lehi when he was called to respond to a house where three boys, around the age of fourteen, had been hanging out together. Somehow, they got hold of a pistol and one of the boys shot another boy and killed him.

Once Jim and his partner arrived to do the investigation, they were told that the mother of the boy who pulled the trigger was working at Wendy's. Jim was instructed by his administration to go to Wendy's and bring the mother home. He was not to tell her much of what had happened. The administration would meet Jim and the mother at her home and break the news. The boy who was shot lived at another house, and his family would soon be informed, as well.

By the time Jim showed up at Wendy's, news had already spread. The mother was somehow aware of the police interaction at her home, but she didn't know anything else. Jim asked the mother to get into the car and he would take her home. As they drove to the home, Jim felt awkward. This was a mother and Jim didn't think that she should be kept in suspense. Certainly he should say something. Anything. So he did.

"An accident has happened with your child," Jim began. "We will tell you more when we get to your home." He left the rest for the administration.

When they got to the home, the mother had formulated an idea as to what had happened. Her suspicions were confirmed when the details of the accident were revealed to her.

Jim left somberly, questioning whether the shooting was intentional or accidental. The case would never be solved.

A BIKE FOR HIS BIRTHDAY

Sometime later, when Jim worked for the police department in Pleasant Grove, he was called to respond to an accident involving a child and a bicycle. It was the boy's eighth birthday and he had just barely received a brand new bike. The boy lived on a slight grade of a hill which made a great run for a shiny, new set of wheels. The boy climbed onto his bicycle and excitedly descended down the road, turning onto the busy street just adjacent to the hill...right into the path of traffic. He was hit and killed instantly by an unsuspecting motorist. When Jim arrived at the accident, he first saw the bike and then the child lying a short distance from his new toy. A shoe had fallen off of the boy's small foot and was lying sideways in the road just a few feet from his body. Jim ignored his sinking feeling, and didn't even allow thoughts of his own precious children enter into his mind. He instinctively found strength and bravely approached the scene. An ambulance soon showed up and the medics immediately tended to the deceased child. While the emergency personnel took care of things on the victim's end, Jim proceeded to obtain information for the accident report, discovering the disheartening details of what had happened. Occasionally, as Jim filled out the paperwork and interviewed the family and witnesses, his thoughts would wander as he caught a glimpse of the boy being covered and taken on a gurney into the ambulance. The small dented bicycle was removed from the road and placed against the curb. Jim quickly redirected his focus back to the tear-stained faces of the victim's survivors and finished the report. As emergency vehicles dispersed, and family returned to their home to discuss a funeral, Jim picked up the bike and took it back to the station to aid in the investigation.

Over time, the bike got moved to the storage area on the north side of the Pleasant Grove Police Department building. The bike sat there for nearly a year.

One day, Jim and some of the other police officers were passing through the storage area when one of the guys picked up the bicycle. "Why do we still have this bike? Hasn't it been here a while?"

"I don't know." Jim shrugged, wondering the same thing.

"Do you even know where it came from?" the officer asked, curiously inspecting the brand new tires and the dents and scratches amidst the new paint on the frame.

Jim disappeared in deep thought for a moment, imagining the excitement of a little boy getting a new bicycle for his birthday. He could almost see the kid rushing to the end of his driveway so he could fearlessly tear down the hill to the bottom of the street. Jim vividly recalled the lifeless body on the road and a forsaken shoe; he shook the memory. "Yeah. I know where it's from." He looked down. "It was an accident and the boy was killed." He stepped towards the bike and gently touched the handle bars. "I guess the family never came for it."

"What do we do with it?" the officer asked.

"I don't know," Jim answered, biting his lip. "They were supposed to come and get it some time ago...perhaps too painful a memory...I don't know." He turned and left the storage unit.

The other officer nodded, solemnly placing the bike back down, deciding to just leave it a little longer.

CHAPTER 4

HAILED A HERO

"An alert Lehi police officer helped an older couple escape their burning home early Thursday morning," the Deseret News article began. Jim never saw the article that published the details of a critical moment that occurred on that cold, early morning. He was just doing his job and was in the right place at the right time doing the right thing.

Working a night shift usually meant working alone. Jim was on grave yard, patrolling neighborhoods at one o'clock in the morning. He drove down 400 East in Lehi and suddenly noticed smoke coming from behind one of the houses. It was mid March, and not unusual to see smoke rolling out of chimneys, but something didn't seem right. He circled back around and stopped in front of the home in question. He studied where the smoke was pouring out and thought, "That's not coming from the chimney!" He got out of his car and cautiously walked through the covered walkway, separating the garage from the house; then he headed into the backyard. Smoke was coming out of the attic. Immediately he ran to the front of the house and knocked on the door of the residents. An elderly gentleman, Frank Huggard, answered.

"Your house is on fire and we need to get you and everybody out," Jim quickly informed. "Who else is inside?"

"It's just me and my wife," Mr. Huggard answered. "We were smelling smoke and I was looking in all the rooms to see where it was coming from."

"It's in the attic. We need to get you out fast." Jim escorted the older couple to the warmth of his patrol car as he alerted the fire department. He was aware that Lehi's fire department consisted of volunteer workers and he knew it might take a while before they arrived. So Jim looked around the yard for a garden hose and then began hooking it up to the house tap. The first fireman arrived in his own car and quickly hopped out.

"Help me get this hose up to the attic," Jim commanded.

The volunteer fireman assisted Jim in getting the vent off the attic where the smoke was coming from. They got the garden hose in and started pouring water in. Soon, several other firemen showed up in their personal vehicles. Eventually, the rest of the fire crew came with the fire truck and took over, successfully containing the blaze. The damage was minimal and no one was injured. Satisfied that things were taken care of, Jim left the scene and finished his shift, patrolling streets. He then drove home and went to bed, not thinking much of the event.

The Next morning, Jim received calls from the administration.

"Hey, the news wants to see you," the sergeant exclaimed.

"What for?" Jim asked, curiously.

"Because of the fire last night," the sergeant answered. "You saved a family and their home."

"Yeah, but isn't that what we do? It's all just a part of our job," Jim answered, modestly.

"Well they want to talk to you. You're a hero, Jim!"

Jim blushed. He'd never really thought of himself as a hero, and he'd never been on the news before. But he conceded and met with Channel 2 News for an interview to tell his story. He'd only been working for the police department for about a year and a half, so he joked with the reporter about the *vast years* of Law Enforcement experience he had. The reporter joked along with him, entertained by Jim's good sense of humor.

It was very fortunate that Jim happened to pass by the Huggard's home that night. Otherwise the house would have quickly become engulfed and the outcome might have been a lot different. Jim was simply happy to be doing his job.

CHAPTER 5

NOT ALWAYS A HERO

There are times when the police have to deal with irrational, outraged, or intoxicated individuals who have made poor choices. Law Enforcement Officers have the arduous task of trying to restore order from chaos in all various circumstances. They confront situations where offenders become angry about their consequences, then accuse the law of being corrupt to get out of their sentences.

Other times, bystanders only witness part of the story involving incidents and misjudge it, pointing their fingers at the police. Although it's not defined in the job description, officers have to endure the harsh and often unfair reviews of society.

BATONS AND TACKLING

Jim was called to respond to a family fight where a man was intoxicated and abusive. When Jim pulled up to the house, the drunken man was trying to leave in his car before the police arrived. Having extremely impaired perception, he backed his vehicle into one of his other cars, also parked in the same driveway.

    Jim was parked in front of the house and noticed that the man's wife was out in the yard. Suddenly, the man got out of his car and tried to go after his wife with rage. Jim jumped out of his patrol car and ordered the woman to go into her house for safety. The husband glanced furiously at Jim then rushed towards him. Jim quickly pulled his baton out with a warning gesture, but the man continued to advance violently towards him. Jim had no other choice but to use the baton on the man, evading his reckless swings. It was the one and only time Jim ever used it. He didn't have a Taser, or a stun gun. None of the officers in his department did. The only option Jim had, to get control of a threatening offender without using his gun, was to use his baton. The drunken man continued attacking Jim when another officer showed up. The officer saw Jim in a standoff with this man and rushed from his car to assist, pulling his baton out. With two officers trying to take this man down, the man fought more furiously. Soon, a third officer showed up, jumped out of his car, and tackled the man. Jim handcuffed the attacker as the third officer held the man down. They eventually hauled him away to jail.

Shortly after the incident, a lady who lived across the street from the abusive man, complained against the third officer because he tackled her neighbor. Jim thought it was interesting that he and the second officer didn't receive any complaints from the woman. Apparently, she didn't see Jim and the second officer using their batons, and she didn't witness the neighbor hurting his wife. She only saw the third officer run from his car and tackle the man.

Often times, the people who complain against police officers don't see or comprehend the whole picture; they misjudge the incident based on incomplete knowledge or biased opinions.

DOMESTIC COMPLAINT

One time, Jim responded to a domestic dispute where a man beat up his wife. Jim ended up arresting the man and taking him to jail but received a complaint for making the arrest. The person that complained was the offender's father, who expressed his dissatisfaction that it wasn't fair. "Why can't you just let him go home?" He insisted that his son didn't do anything, even though there was valid evidence that he had beat up his wife. The father was a city employee who was angry that the city would consider arresting *his* son. After all, he worked for the same organization that the police did and thought that the city should have allegiance to their employees.

Jim couldn't believe it. He thought: *Your son just got through beating his wife up. That's why he's going to jail...because he did something wrong.*

No ranks or titles should give anyone the liberty to get away with crime. Nevertheless, Jim got a complaint because he arrested a man, who committed a misdemeanor, and took him to jail.

Other minor complaints Jim received were because he told things how they were. He didn't mince words, but spoke direct and up front. Jim didn't like to sugar coat explanations or beat around the bush. He was a *matter-of-fact* kind of guy who dealt with people straight forward. But many people like you to sugar coat things. They don't like the straight forward approach. He was more honest with his opinions when he told someone that their irrational behavior was ridiculous instead of telling them that it probably wasn't the best thing to get drunk and drive or whatever they were doing irresponsibly. So, offenders complained, not because Jim did something wrong or bad, but because of how he said it and people took offense.

CHAPTER 6

HUMOR IN THE FORCE

Although Jim took his job seriously, he had a humorous side to him. Harmless jokes and pranks lightened up the workplace, adding a tension breaker to the perilous pressures that he and his fellow officers often had to face.

Jim's friends with the police force reached far past the boundaries of the department he worked for. And the jokes extended to neighboring cities, where other officers, from surrounding police departments, played friendly games back and forth with each other.

TOILET PAPERING THE POLICE WAY

Certainly, it is never a good idea to litter or become a public nuisance, but many people like to engage in an innocuous toilet papering prank, decorating the houses and trees, of friends, with the endless paper garland.

The guys at Jim's department used a different kind of garland. They would take crime scene tape and place it at night around the front doors of a neighboring police department. Often they would include an old unmarked patrol car in the gag, parking it in front of the doors within the boundaries of the police tape. The other departments knew it was just a friendly joke from Jim's department.

Jim and the other officers were disappointed, once when the only retaliation that came from one of the neighboring recipients was crime scene tape wrapped around their flag pole. Jim thought: *Is that the best you can do?* He shrugged, guessing that they weren't much for pranks.

ALARMS AND AIRHORNS

Once, late at night, Jim and his partner, both on patrol but in different cars, responded to an alarm at the city shops. The city complex had an open compound area and when they arrived, they noticed that one of the bay doors was open.

The other officer got out of his car and approached Jim's car. "That's spooky," he remarked.

"I guess we ought to check it out," Jim suggested.

The other officer nodded, stepping into the darkness towards the open bay door. Jim slowly drove his patrol car behind his partner as they both looked around, in all directions, for anyone who might have broken in. Jim's buddy entered the open bay area and cautiously walked through the middle of the compound, searching. Jim couldn't see anyone in sight. It looked as though it would be a false alarm. He watched his partner continue to pan the property. Suddenly, Jim couldn't resist. Seeing his buddy standing there in the dark was too much for him. He pulled his patrol car up close behind the officer and honked his air horn. That scared him. Jim knew it was a dumb thing to do if a prowler was there, but he was convinced there was no danger. Besides, at the time it seemed funny watching his friend jump out of his skin with an unmatchable expression of terror. Jim laughed until his stomach hurt. His friend cast a hard glance at him, his mouth gaping as if to say, "How could you do that?" This only made Jim laugh harder. The other officer shook his head and cracked a grin at the spectacle of his partner.

THINGS THAT GO BUMP IN THE NIGHT

One cold night in December of 1992, Jim was on a graveyard shift, patrolling streets. His mind was heavily occupied with the recent tragedy of Trooper Joseph Brumett.

A few weeks earlier, on the morning of December 11, Trooper Brumett was dispatched to an accident that occurred on Interstate 15, involving several vehicles. He was a young dedicated officer, just 24 years old, and had only been with the Utah Highway Patrol for merely 9 months. Regardless of his meager tenure, he impressed his peers and performed as a veteran.

The morning of the tragedy, Officer Brumett began directing traffic and clearing debris from the perilous roadway where the multiple car accident had taken place. It was during the 7 a.m. commute, which only heightened the danger. Despite the cold and bitter weather Joey, as he was often called, persisted in keeping the traffic flowing, slowly but steadily. Suddenly a pickup truck struck Trooper Brumett, and then continued on hitting another vehicle. The driver jumped out of his truck and fled the scene on foot. He was an undocumented immigrant who was eventually found hiding in a nearby warehouse. He was arrested, and convicted of hit-and-run and driving without a license. Trooper Brumett was airlifted to a hospital in Salt Lake City but had died at the scene, leaving behind his new wife of only one year. "Trooper Joey Brumett; Utah Highway Patrol; Killed in the Line of Duty" was etched upon his gravestone, along with a smaller Utah plaque: "That We May Never Forget". Jim was really affected by the untimely death of Trooper Joey Brumett. He was killed in the line duty, doing the same thing Jim did.

Thoughts of Trooper Brumett consumed Jim's mind as he patrolled the abandoned streets of Lehi after dark. Part of his routine included driving around to the schools, checking the doors and windows to make sure they were secure. Jim pulled into the elementary school's parking lot and continued on behind the back of the building where the portables were. Jim's coworker, Alec, who was on swing shift, often joined Jim patrolling streets when their shifts crossed. Alec spotted Jim entering the lot of the elementary school that night and decided to play a joke on him. As Jim drove behind the school, Alec parked his patrol car where Jim wouldn't see it, then got out and hid.

Meanwhile, Jim climbed out of his car and checked the doors and windows of the school. When things looked secure, he got back into his patrol car and headed back around to the front of the school, still thinking of Trooper Brumett. As Jim's car crossed the parking lot and approached the exit, Alec jumped out of his hiding spot and pounded on the back of Jim's patrol car. Jim nearly jumped out of his seat. He slammed on his brakes. "What in the world just happened?" His heart seemed to stop then start again at a full, fast pounding.

Jim's fellow officer rushed towards the car window, breaking the dark silence with his laughter. "Gotcha!" he hollered with satisfaction, opening Jim's car door. Suddenly his look of glory turned to concern as he stared back into Jim's pale face. "Hey, are you okay?"

Jim rubbed his forehead and blew out a long breath. "Yeah, I'm fine."

"I guess I got you good...it was only a joke..."

Jim looked at his buddy and graced a subtle smile. "No problem. I was just thinking of Trooper Brumett...you know, the accident and all...and then when you hit the car, I got spooked."

His buddy looked down solemnly. "Hey, I'm sorry. If I'd known, I never would have..."

"Don't worry," Jim chuckled and the color in his face began to return. "I'm always good for a joke...I'm just relieved that it was only a joke." He reassuringly patted his partner on the arm.

MANNEQUINS AND MISCHIEF

Shane Packer was a true blue prankster. He was an officer that worked with Jim who liked to play around and have a good time. Somehow Shane came across a mannequin that satisfied hours of jokes and laughs. He would dress up the mannequin in random street clothes, and then when it was dark he would place it randomly in the backseat of one of his fellow officers' patrol cars. When the unknowing officer would get into his car, he would be met with the surprise guest.

Shane enjoyed surprising people, pulling pranks on them when they least expected it. He especially enjoyed working the night shifts which provided ample opportunities to place the mannequin in different places around the city, on benches, near street poles, or in front of businesses that were closed down for the night. He loved to try and spook the other officers on night patrol. Sometimes they didn't know if they were checking out a real person or just one of Shane's mannequin characters that night.

Jim remembers one time when he aided Shane in a prank. They took the mannequin to a closed Subway restaurant in Lehi. After placing the dummy in front of the store in a suspicious position, they hid around the corner to watch for the other officer on duty drive by. Jim and Shane anxiously waited for something to happen. The officer did pass the store, but he wouldn't take the bait. It was very disappointing. Certainly, they had to be careful with their jokes. They didn't want to go too far with them or else the wrong people might see the suspicious mannequin...and call the police.

THE MASK

When Jim was working at the Pleasant Grove Police Department, somebody acquired a rubber mask. It was a spooky character Halloween mask that had the realistic features of a person. Some of the guys would place the mask on one of their CPR dummies, and then situate it in different places throughout the station. Any particular day, you might enter a room and be surprised to see the strange figure standing there in the dark corner, or sitting on the chair at your desk. It was always dressed in different street clothes each time it was set, and placed in positions to appear as though it was sleeping, writing a report or leaning against a wall.

Their favorite spot to place the dummy was in the dispatch center. At night, one of the officers would sneak the dummy into a holding cell next to the dispatch center when the dispatcher was turned around and looking the other way. The officer would press the face of the mask up against the glass window of the door. It was so realistic that it appeared as if somebody was actually standing there in the holding cell. Eventually, the dispatcher would turn around and catch a glimpse of the face before screaming. Even when it happened more than once the dummy would catch them off guard, because they didn't know when to expect it.

The dummy was moved around randomly throughout the building. Once, somebody put it in the chief's chair in his office after he had gone home for the night. When the chief returned to the station early in the morning, he entered his dark room and turned on the light. He was startled to see someone sitting in his chair, but he was a good sport.

THE PHANTOM RADIO

When the dummies weren't enough, Shane would take a hand radio and switch it to a non working regular station. Then he would place the radio underneath the backseat of one of the other officer's car. Sometime during the day, while the officer was on patrol, Shane would call out the officer's name on the radio and speak as if he was someone sitting in the back seat. The officer was always surprised, and quite humored by Shane's pranks.

MUG SHOTS

In Lehi there were only a total of about 10 officers in the department. Five or six of them worked the road together. If there were 500 people in a police department, it was nearly impossible to get to know everyone. With Lehi's small force, they became a pretty tight-knit group and goofed around like brothers would. Four of them, particularly, liked to dress up, but not for Halloween. Jim was one of the four guys that enjoyed dressing in wild attire and taking mug shots with various goofy poses. On one occasion, the four officers put on mullet wigs and bandanas then went cruising around in an old white Ford Fairmont. They drove to American Fork and stopped at a café, conspicuously sitting out in the parking lot. They were hoping to get a reaction but, strangely, nobody seemed to care. It was odd to the officers but perhaps it was more normal than they realized. They left for home, disappointed. All that effort and nobody noticed.

RUBBER SNAKE

When Jim was in Pleasant Grove, he found a rubber snake at some store and purchased it for a future gag. One evening, when Jim was working the swing shift, he backed up a traffic stop for Officer Gerald Sutherland. Gerald had stopped a car and was speaking with the driver.

While Gerald was occupied, getting the driver's license and registration, Jim stuffed the snake in his hand and casually walked towards his partner's patrol car. He opened the door and slipped the rubber snake on the seat, then sauntered back to his own car and got in.

Jim watched patiently from his front row view.

Gerald began to walk back to his car to run a check on the driver he stopped. He glanced at Jim and waved, acknowledging his presence.

Jim smiled and waved back, trying not to let his grin give anything away.

Gerald opened his door and nearly sat down, but he caught himself.

Jim snickered.

Gerald took a second look, with his mouth gaping open. He shot a glance towards Jim and raised his brow.

Jim waved again, blushing under his laughter.

Gerald cracked a smile and just shook his head as he flipped the rubber snake into the backseat. He was a good sport when it came to jokes, and a great officer. Only a few years later he would become the Chief of Police in Pleasant Grove.

CALL A COP

During Jim's first year as a full time officer in Lehi, Melanie was pregnant with their last child. The baby was due around the time of the Lehi roundup, when the police department was extremely busy. All the officers were on duty during that big event.

Being new to the job, Jim didn't want to risk his position, so he didn't dare ask for any time off in excess of what he was allotted. Before he left for work on the days of the roundup, he would tell her, "You can't call me if you go into labor because I'll be on duty."

"What?" Melanie scrunched her brow in astonishment.

"You know I'm new on the force..." Jim reminded.

"Yeah but what do I do? Call a cop?" Melanie jested.

"Sure." Jim shrugged. "Maybe they'll send me..."

Melanie rolled her eyes and thought, "I can see it now. I'll go into labor, call the cops and probably get that officer who is *so* dramatic... you know, the one who acts like *Nervous Nellie* all the time. Sure, he's super nice and all, if you don't mind someone who is easily stressed out. With my luck, he'll pick me up, take me to the hospital and end up delivering this baby on the way there, after having a nervous breakdown."

Fortunately for Melanie, she didn't go into labor until after the roundup when Jim could accompany her.

HEAD PRINTS

When Shane was up to his old tricks again, Jim assisted him in a brilliant prank. The Lehi chief of police at the time was Richard Hill. He was a down-to-earth, upright man that fulfilled his responsibilities seriously and articulately.

Shane got a fingerprint card and altered it a bit, creating the first ever *forehead print card*, complete with instructions. Then he placed the packet in an official FBI envelope and gave it the appearance of being sent in the mail from the agency.

Shane and Jim delivered the special envelope to Chief Hill as if it had come in the mail. The chief took the packet to his office and reviewed the instructions of implementing forehead prints.

After a short while, Chief Hill dashed out of his office, in a panic, and explained to Shane and Jim about the new personal identification cards. "Hey, I need to start doing these new forehead prints now and I've got to present the new program to the rest of the department."

Shane and Jim couldn't contain themselves. They burst into laughter, giving the joke away. Chief Hill caught on, embarrassed at first; but he was a good sport. Shaking his head in dismay, he pressed the *head print packet* against Shane's vibrating stature, and returned to his office. Shane was laughing too hard to grab the packet before it fell to the floor, which made him laugh harder.

DRINKING ON THE JOB

When Jim was working for the Orem Police Department, Officer Brian Randall was the jokester. One morning, Brian had just finished working grave yard and Jim was coming on for the day duty. Beginning a shift always meant briefing, where the officers starting the new shift would be updated as to what had happened previously and what they should be aware of. Jim had gathered in the meeting room at the station with about ten other guys who also happened to be new to the department; some had only been there about a week. None of them were familiar with Brian Randall.

When Brian sauntered into the room, in full uniform, just coming off shift, he casually passed through the congregation of other officers, holding a can of beer. Naturally, an officer holding a can of beer stirred a little curiosity. Brian sat down amidst the men and began striking up a little conversation.

After a minute or two, Brian glanced at the can in his hand. "You know, I'm kind of thirsty." He popped the drink open and took a swig.

The other officers were too stunned to say anything. They just looked around, exchanging surprised glances.

Brian took another swallow, bigger this time, and wiped his mouth with his sleeve. He looked up at a couple of the officers, "Hey, you want one? I got more out in the car."

Everyone continued to just sit there, frozen in shock.

Jim thought: *Serious? You're gonna lose your job.*

After a while, and to the relief of all the officers, Brian finally revealed his joke. Grinning, he took hold of the top of the can and pulled a Pepsi out of the beer shell. He had cut the top off of an empty beer can and dropped the Pepsi inside so it appeared as if he was drinking beer. It looked quite legitimate. Although Jim and some of the other officers thought it was kind of funny, the lieutenant didn't think so.

CHAPTER 7

GUNS, KNIVES AND PIPE BENDERS

Jim never knew what to expect on any given call he was dispatched to. His experiences were inconsistent, yet they invariably taught him how dangerous his job truly was. He also learned how creative criminals could be in their personal challenges.

GUN RACKING

At the first of Jim's career, there was a man who was an alcoholic whom Jim visited on a semi regular basis, due to the trouble he would get into. One day, Jim and his partner were dispatched to the duplex where their erratic pal lived, but on this occasion it was the threat of suicide. As they arrived and headed towards the front door, they could hear the man speaking to the dispatcher from the covered carport where a side door allowed a second entrance into the home. It sounded as if the dispatcher was trying to talk the man out of killing himself. The man was standing just outside his door and out of view. Jim nodded for his partner to follow him towards the carport. Suddenly, Jim heard the racking of a gun. His eyes widened and he glanced at his partner who was equally surprised.

"Let's get out of here," Jim uttered under his breath.

The two officers immediately retreated, and headed for the other side of the street where Jim had parked his car. They called for backup and the assistance of other agencies to get the situation underhand. After all was said and done, the man denied having a gun, although a rifle was found in his home.

Jim never forgot hearing the action of the gun from behind the carport and thinking: *Wow...this is for real*. Jim knew very well that when you have any suspicion that a gun is present, you don't question it. Hearing the action of that gun that day gave him the startling realization that this was the *real deal*. Although you seem to be aware of the danger and risk as you are training to become a police officer, it doesn't really hit you until you confront a possible life-threatening situation, dead on. Little did Jim know that this incident would be the first of many he would encounter with guns, well before his shootout in 2002.

GUN IN A TREE

While working for the Lehi Police Department, Jim responded to a domestic disturbance where a guy, presumably, had a gun. When Jim got to the house, he assisted other agencies in searching around the property and neighborhood for the man. There were several big trees surrounding the house, and in the dark the officers were having great difficulty finding the man in suspicion. Finally, the officers regrouped, gathering at a spot in front of the house to decide what to do. A little bit of time passed, as they waited for everyone to gather. As Jim was standing amidst the officers, one of the last men to join the group happened to look up, discovering the man they were looking for. He had been hiding in the large tree above them. Fortunately, the man didn't have a gun on him at that time, but Jim learned a valuable lesson. If the man happened to have had a gun in his possession, he could have taken out several of the officers easily before anybody would have realized what was happening. From that day forward, whenever Jim was involved with any hot situations, he'd look in the area and then take a quick glance in all the trees, just in case. Some people thought he was crazy looking up in trees, but Jim's eyes had been opened and he knew it was a possibility. He understood that unseen circumstances could mean the difference between life and death. Being alert to details was important in this job.

GANGS ON STATE STREET

There was a time when Jim was patrolling in Orem and he received a call from dispatch that two cars were chasing each other on State Street. He located the two cars and was able to pull one of them over to a road, just off of State Street.

The evening was late and the sky dark. As Jim climbed out of his patrol car and approached the other vehicle, he could tell there were four people inside. Jim recognized the driver. He was a young man from one of the gangs running around in Orem. Jim saw him quite frequently, either in casual passing, or during legitimate run-ins the kid had with the law. Jim had a pretty good rapport with him, due to their confrontations, and also due to the fact that the kid liked to talk, perhaps a little bit too much. This was a benefit for Jim, because he would learn tips and insights that proved to be valuable for specific cases.

"Hey Cal. Fancy seeing you again." Jim raised his brow and cast a subtle smile. "May I see your license and registration?"

Cal looked up at Jim and said, "Yeah, um..hey...let me talk to you for a second. I kind of need to tell you somethin'." He tossed his head slightly to his left, gesturing to speak outside of the car.

"Okay." Jim nodded and got him out of the vehicle, leading him towards his patrol car. Jim leaned against the hood. "What's up?"

Cal stepped closer to Jim and spoke quietly. "There's a gun here. I'm just tellin' ya....y'know. It's gonna be underneath Emilio's seat. That's where you'll find it...he's the guy sitting on the left side in the back." He pursed his lips and nodded confidently. "So...yeah."

Jim's jaw dropped, but he kept his composure. "Thanks, Cal. I appreciate this, a lot."

Cal nodded. "Oh...and don't tell him I said nothin'."

"Sure," Jim agreed then escorted Cal back to the car. He peered into the window. "Hey, guys. I just need you to wait here for a few minutes." The other men nodded, cooperatively.

Jim went back to his car, called for backup, then waited. Ultimately, when backup arrived, all the men in Cal's car were pulled out of the vehicle. One of the officers checked underneath the seat where Emilio was sitting and, sure enough, there was a pistol.

Earlier, when Jim had turned his lights on to pull the car over, Emilio was desperately trying to figure out what he was going to do with the gun. He decided to hide it, and stuck it down under his seat so the police wouldn't catch him with it.

All four of the men were gang members. One of the officers ran a report on each of them and showed it to Jim. "Hey. This guy, Emilio, he's going to prison. Look at his report!"

Jim skimmed over the information and swallowed hard, knowing what might have happened if he had not have been warned about the gun. He was sure that the reason Cal squealed was because of the friendship he had with him.

Jim looked over at Cal, who was sitting on the curb near one of the police cars, and nodded his head in a gesture to thank him again. Cal, who had been carefully observing Jim, raised a brow and nodded back.

EXPIRED PLATE

Jim knew a guy, Frank, from business licensing that he became good friends with. They would occasionally ride together in Jim's car. Frank would do his business licensing checks and Jim would do his patrolling and ordinance work. Strangely enough, when they were together, it seemed like Jim would always come across some interesting situations.

One day, while they were driving about, Jim noticed a truck looking a little peculiar. He saw the stickers were outdated so he ran a license plate check, discovering it was expired.

"Frank," Jim informed his friend, casually, "it looks like we are pulling this guy over."

"Alright." Frank shrugged, wondering what might be in store this time.

Jim turned his lights on until the driver of the truck pulled off to the side of the road. Jim stopped behind the truck and got out of his car. As he approached the driver, he noticed there was a gun inside the cab, on one side of the truck.

The driver noticed Jim eyeing the gun. "Oh...I just got back from camping. I've been hunting...you know."

Jim smiled. "Okay. May I see your license and registration?" The man handed over what was requested then Jim ran a report.

Jim was surprised at the findings. The driver had numerous warrants out for him and he was unlawfully in possession of a gun. He arrested the man, in awe that he found him, all because he had an expired license plate.

OPEN CARRY AT THE UNIVERSITY

Carrying a firearm, publicly, in plain sight is known as *open carry*. *Concealed carry* is where the firearm cannot be seen by an observer. Open carry laws for handguns vary in the United States, depending on the state. In Utah, a license is required in order for someone to openly carry a loaded firearm. No license is required when the weapon is unloaded and exposed. For the gun to be classified as unloaded it must not have a round in the firing position, and must have at least two mechanical actions, or safety catches. Also, the firearm must clearly be visible at all times.

Around the time when open carry policies had been approved in Utah, an incident occurred on the Utah Valley University campus. The campus police confronted a man who was carrying a pistol in a holster. They asked the man to leave the area, in which he did. Shortly afterward, Jim was dispatched to Main Street and University Parkway. The same man who had been carrying a gun on the grounds of the university was seen walking down the sidewalk. Jim and his partner were the first ones to locate him. Jim looked at the man who was dressed in a t-shirt and jeans. He was an ordinary college boy, and didn't give any impression that he was trying to cause any trouble.

"We'd like to talk to you about your gun," Jim began. "Is it loaded?"

"No, Sir." The man shifted back and forth, and nervously brushed his fingers across the handle of his weapon.

"Mind if I see it?" Jim stated more than asked.

"Alright." The man pulled the pistol from his holster and handed it to Jim.

Jim checked and confirmed that it wasn't loaded. "Nice looking gun."

The man grinned, proudly shoving his hands in his back pockets.

Jim handed the gun back to the man, and cast a serious look. "You're not breaking the law," Jim assured. "But it's not real wise carrying a firearm that's not concealed or the police will get called every time. Especially, around schools, considering the recent shootings on school ground.

"Yes, Sir." The man nodded.

The young college student was compliant. Jim didn't want to arrest the man, but if he had been defiant, the outcome might have been different. It was a matter of clarifying the situation and assuring that citizens in the community were safe. It wasn't a common thing for someone to be walking down the sidewalk with a gun out in the open and it made people rightfully nervous. Citizens had every right to be concerned, especially around school grounds. School shootings in the United States have occurred as early as 1850 when a teacher was killed in West Chester Pennsylvania by a man hiding in the woods near the school.

Numerous incidents involving guns on school property have occurred since then; some resulting very tragically. In December, 2012, Sandy Hook elementary school endured a mass shooting where 20 children and 6 adults were killed. Within approximately one year after that horrific day, 44 U.S. school shootings occurred, resulting in 28 deaths.

One of the worst college campus incidents was the Virgina Tech shooting in Blacksburg, Virginia in April, 2007. The gunman killed 32 people and wounded 17 before committing suicide.

Whenever Jim was called to check out a firearm sighting, Jim would ask the owner if he could hold the gun until they were done discussing the matter. This assured the safety of both the officer and the citizen. People in Utah County were good about cooperating, and issues were usually worked out peacefully.

Once, when Jim worked in Lehi, he made a traffic stop where the driver had a concealed weapon and a permit to go with it. He asked the man to give him his gun while they were discussing the traffic violation. The man kindly abided, handing a huge pistol over. Jim's eyes widened and he chuckled at the size of that weapon.

FELONY STOP

Only a couple weeks after Jim's first shootout in 2002, he was called to a fight that broke out at one of the parks. As Jim approached the location, he saw one of the vehicles leaving and he was soon informed that there was a gun involved. Jim followed the van then pulled it over. With a gun involved, Jim did a "felony stop" where he used his PA to tell the people to get out of their car, put their hands up, and get on the ground. There were 2 people in the van. They stepped out of their vehicle and lay on the ground. When backup arrived, Jim and the other officers searched the men, finding a gun on one of them. The men were handcuffed and taken to the station for questioning.

Jim's sergeant, who was present, looked at him and said, "Flygare, you keep coming across these gun incidents, in just the last couple weeks." Jim ended up getting an officer of the month award, most likely for handling so many dangerous situations safely, professionally and responsibly.

APARTMENT SHOTGUN

Shortly after the gun incident at the park, Jim was called to the apartments across the freeway from Utah Valley University, to respond to a threat involving a man with a shotgun. As Jim arrived at the complex, one of the other officers exclaimed, "Jim's here! We'll be fine, now."

Jim felt great satisfaction that his department trusted him so greatly. Truthfully, he never felt any more skilled than any of the other officers on his public safety team. He was just doing his job, like everyone else he worked with. Ultimately, Jim and the officers apprehended the man with the gun.

THE PENNSYLVANIA DEAL

Jim once read an article in the newspaper about a stabbing that occurred in 2014, at a high school located in Pennsylvania. A 16-year-old student took two 8-inch steel blade knives and went on a stabbing frenzy, wounding 21 students and a security guard before being tackled by an assistant principal. Apparently, during the chaos, somebody had pulled the fire alarm. Jim couldn't understand what they might have been thinking when they pulled the alarm supposing everyone would evacuate and get out of the building safely. Instead, it caused everyone to gather closer in around the attacker, allowing him to stab more people in one place. Jim thought it was a good intention but a bad choice with lethal consequences. Perhaps Jim was able to see the blunder so evidently because of his avid training and experience.

A KNIFE IN BUSINESS

Once, Jim was dispatched to a business where a man was having a dispute with the store owners.

The man was a customer, but had caused trouble and was asked to leave. When he refused to go, he became aggressive and the police were called.

Jim entered the building and assessed the situation, discovering that the man was out of line.

"You need to leave the store," Jim pressed.

The guy stared at Jim for a moment then whipped out a pocket knife.

Jim was surprised. The man didn't seem like the type to pull a knife. Instinctively, Jim grabbed for the arm holding the knife, but the man jerked away before Jim could get a secure grip.

Jim retreated back a few steps, out of stabbing reach. He thought: *Oh, man! Now what?* He didn't want to grab for his arm again, because he knew he was likely to get stabbed on the second try. The owners were still standing within close range of the attacker and Jim was unsure of what the man's next move was. This irrational customer was apparently the unpredictable type and Jim feared he could take a stab at any one of them. Jim pulled out his gun. "Put the knife down!"

The man took one look at the gun and thrust his knife against his own wrist. He didn't cut himself, but he held the knife like he was threatening to.

Jim commanded the man to put the knife down again, but the man refused. Jim repeated himself two or three times until finally, after a few minutes of urgent persuading, the man put the knife down. Jim handcuffed him and hauled him off to the hospital where he could be evaluated for psychological problems.

PIPE BENDER

On another occasion, Jim got called to a fight occurring at a residence. Two men were having a heavy disagreement when things turned violent.

When Jim arrived at the home, he was quite surprised. One of the men was holding a two-foot-long pipe bender. He had smacked the other man on the back with it. Jim figured that during the fight, the perpetrator must have just grabbed whatever he could get his hands onto then took out his rage on the other guy with his newly obtained weapon.

After apprehending the weapon, Jim inspected the injured man's back and was aghast. The offender had hit this man so hard, that it left the imprint of the pipe on his back. Obviously, there was no dispute about what had happened, and the attacker went to jail.

CROWBAR

Another unusual incident occurred when Jim responded to a fight at a trailer park where a man was threatening to injure another man. When Jim and his partner pulled up to the scene in his patrol car, he saw a man standing outside of the trailer where the incident was occurring. The other man involved in the argument went inside the trailer. Exhibiting rage, the man outside picked up a crowbar, and headed towards the front door of the trailer, ready to use the weapon on his foe.

Still in his patrol car, Jim quickly rolled down the window, and yelled as loud as he could, "Put it down, now!"

The man caught sight of the police officers for the first time and immediately dropped the crowbar. He had been so angry; he hadn't seen them until now.

Jim blew out a sigh of relief, grateful the man was so quick to comply. Certainly, the situation could have involved a more distressing outcome, requiring physical interaction of the police officers. Jim and his partner got out of the car and followed through with what needed to be done to resolve the incident.

FILLETED

Calls for disputes were increasingly numerous and grievously common. Jim responded to a home where two male roommates had been arguing. One of the men finally grabbed a knife and sliced his roommate along the length of his forearm then took off running. When Jim arrived, the injured roommate was huddled on the floor, holding his bleeding arm against his body. Jim bent down to check the man's wound and gasped. The victim's arm was literally filleted. Jim kept the man calm and secured his deep cut until an ambulance came. Ultimately, they did find the attacker, but Jim struggled to forget the images of such a horrific wound.

KICKED IN THE HEAD

Jim showed up to a restaurant one evening, where he was dispatched concerning a fight that was occurring just outside of a local café. As soon as Jim got to the scene, he learned quickly what it was all about. A woman was on the ground, and her outraged boyfriend was hitting and kicking her, repetitively. This man managed to kick his girlfriend in the head a few times before Jim was able to stop him. Jim arrested the attacker and called an ambulance to take the woman to the hospital. As time went on, Jim sadly learned that the woman, who had been kicked, sustained permanent nerve damage in part of her face. Her lips and chin had lost feeling from the afflictions she received that evening. Jim was grateful he could intervene, to prevent a worse fate.

Unfortunately, Jim saw similar scenes frequently. As a public safety worker, he helped people and apprehended those who were causing pain and affliction on others. It was consoling for him to know that he could make a difference in their lives; that's what kept him going when things got tough.

HAMMER HITTER

One evening, in Lehi, Jim got called to a family fight. He approached the house where the dispute was occurring and leaned towards the front door with his ear. Often, Jim found that by listening before knocking, he could learn a lot about the situation. Sometimes it would reveal the truth behind closed doors, as he could hear clamoring or yelling.

Jim waited for a moment, and could hear arguing. Then suddenly he heard somebody scream, like they had been hurt. Jim's eyes widened. Normally he didn't just barge in, but this time he did because of the suspicion of imminent danger. He thrust the door open and ran into the home, assessing where the commotion was coming from. The family was in the kitchen, but as soon as Jim had appeared, everyone froze, trying to give the impression that nothing was happening and everything was fine.

One man had a hammer in his hand. "Hey! What's happening?" he greeted, congenially.

"That's what I would like to know." Jim was still catching his breath after dashing into the house. He looked directly at the hammer. "Are you fixing something?"

"Fixing to go to jail," a girl muttered. "He hit me with it!" As it turned out, the girl was the sister to the assaulter. Jim dealt with everyone, and then hauled the hammer hitter to jail. That was one of the few times he actually heard someone scream as he arrived to a scene.

Of all the domestic disputes, Jim was most saddened by incidents where children were present and witnessed everything. It was traumatically disturbing to their young hearts and minds.

According to studies throughout the United States, the repercussions of home-based violent acts could affect children their entire lives, leading to emotional, social, behavioral, and physical problems. To a child, a home is supposed to be a place of security and comfort. When these beliefs are violated, children let go of their ability to trust or have confidence. The studies have concluded that there are approximately 3 to 10 million children every year that witness domestic violence in their homes. These studies have also indicated that when children are exposed to such incidents, they are at a higher risk of being abused or neglected.

BEAT AND NEARLY DROWNED

Jim was called to a domestic dispute where a husband had punched his wife. As Jim spoke with the woman, he learned that, a week earlier, her husband had tried to drown her. She was taking a bath and he attempted to strangle her. Jim arrested the man and not only charged him with assault, but also brought to the court's attention the husband's previous attempt to drown his wife.

CHAPTER 8

THE ULTIMATE SACRIFICE

Police officers dedicate their lives to the community, helping to provide safe and happy environments for the public to live in. These public service workers also put their lives on the line, taking on dangerous jobs that prove their true valor. On occasion, precarious assignments turn into life-threatening events, where valiant police officers may suffer fatal consequences. Such was the incident that took place in 2012 when officers from the Narcotics Strike Force approached a small house in Ogden, Utah.

Earlier, in December of 2011, agents had attempted a knock-and-talk, where an officer knocked on the door of the home to speak with a man suspected of growing marijuana inside his residence.

There was no response and the police considered that perhaps this property was a grow house, vacant but used specifically to grow marijuana. While the agents were trying to contact the suspect at this time, they observed that marijuana cultivation was evident, and so they pursued a "knock-and-announce" daytime search warrant, that was ultimately obtained in January of 2012.

The team of officers returned to the grow house on Wednesday, January 4th, with their warrant, and proceeded to enter into the property so heavily involved in illegal activity.

Roy police officer, Jason Vanderwarf, was the first to knock on the wooden door and announce their presence on that cold January evening around 8:45 p.m. "Police, search warrant!" he yelled, as required. There was no answer. He repeated his knock and announce several times, giving about a half a minute in between each knock.

Other officers joined in yelling, "Police, search warrant!" Most of them were wearing only soft body armor instead of the heavier entry gear, having no reason to believe higher protection was needed since this particular suspect's record was rated at a lower risk level, consisting of only misdemeanors. Other officers weren't even wearing any protective covering over their police attire.

Finally, after receiving no response to their official greeting, they decided to enter the building to see if they could locate the suspect and serve his drug search warrant. The officers gained entry into the house, and though they believed it was uninhabited since they never saw any signs of activity, they still announced their presence, loudly. Still, there was no response from the owner. For several minutes after the initial entry, they continued to announce themselves as they started to clear the home.

The team split up, with half of the group going downstairs, and the other half staying upstairs. Agent Vanderwarf led the split to the basement, soon discovering the marijuana plants, an artificial light and a watering system, confirming, without a doubt, the team's suspicions of illegal drug activity.

Ogden police officer, Shane Grogan, remained upstairs and entered a small hallway near the kitchen. He yelled, "Police, search warrant!" then saw a hand, holding a Beretta Storm 9mm pistol, appear around the door. The gun fired immediately, hitting officer Grogan in the cheek. He staggered into an adjacent bathroom and returned fire with his 40-caliber Glock pistol.

Ogden police officer, Derek Draper, who was situated behind Grogan, also fired. He was not aware that officer Grogan had been hit at this point, but he continued to shoot as bullets buzzed through his hair. Both officers emptied their guns, and crossfire stopped as the perpetrator moved positions.

Officer Draper jumped behind a wall, taking cover in the kitchen. Officer Grogan lurched unsteadily after him, only to fall on top of him. "Are you okay?" Officer Draper asked. Officer Grogan was holding his face. He pulled his hand away, revealing the bullet wound. Officer Draper immediately switched into rescue mode, pulling his critically injured companion out of the house and yelling for other officers to *get out*. The shooting continued as the gunman fiercely fired upon the policemen who were attempting to exit the home.

When Agent Vanderwarf heard the shooting from the basement, he ran upstairs, only to witness Ogden police officer Kasey Burell hit the floor, his face covered in blood, having been shot in the head by the gunman. Officer Burell was also hit, in the abdomen. Ogden police officer, Jared Francom, did his best to cover officer Burell, even though he had been hit as well.

Agent Vanderwarf started towards the two wounded officers, but he didn't get far. The gunman shot agent Vanderwarf in the hip. Vanderwarf fell down the basement stairs and quickly assessed his wound. He was definitely hit, but mobile. Hearing the unceasing gunfire upstairs only motivated him to get back up and help his comrades. He ran up the stairs and towards the two injured officers, dodging gunfire along the way. As he reached his fellow officers, he witnessed the Weber County Sheriff Sergeant, Nate Hutchinson, get hit.

Officer Michael Rounkles, who was patrolling in the area, had heard the call and responded to the scene. He attempted to enter the house to help pull the wounded officers out. It was like a battle field and Officer Rounkles was shot, by the gunman, in his mouth and forearm.

Officer Draper helped officer Grogan to safety then returned to assist Agent Vanderwarf and Sergeant Hutchinson, who were dragging Officers Francom and Burrell out. The gunman stepped to the doorway and continued to fire after them. Officers, surrounding the house, returned fire. The gunman finally retreated back into his home, but not before causing further destruction. Sergeant Hutchinson was shot again, having been hit in his rib and his side and in both arms. Officer Francom had been shot six times. Two injuries were internal and one entered his back, severing his spine.

Neighbors around the spectacle had heard the gunfire and ran out of their homes to see what was going on. Officers surrounding the horrific scene, yelled for the spectators to get back into their houses and get down.

The gunman slipped out of a back bedroom window and took refuge in an aluminum shed just behind the house. New officers on the scene pursued the gunman, surrounding the shed. They yelled for him to come out with his hands up, and exchanged fire with the relentless gunman. Finally, after getting wounded, the attacker surrendered, leaving a bloody aftermath amidst his illegal marijuana growing operation. Five officers had received serious injuries, and one was dead. Agent Jared Francom left behind a wife and two young children.

The gunman, Matthew Stewart, was charged with aggravated murder and six counts of attempted aggravated murder, among other things. He was a 37 year old army veteran who suffered from post-traumatic stress disorder, depression and anxiety. He was against the government and disliked the police, revealing to a friend that if the police ever came to his house, he would go out shooting and not let them take him alive.

Some gunmen shoot once only to realize, in terror, what they have done. There was never any remorse from Matthew Stewart for the bloodshed and destruction that he caused, and nobody seemed to be aware that this suspect was emotionally loaded and ready to blow.

The officers didn't know what their fate would be when they delivered a drug warrant to a small quiet house in Ogden on that dark January evening. But that is the life of law enforcement officers. They perform every assignment, never knowing if they will come home alive. Most of them selflessly risk their lives and demonstrate compassion that more than qualifies them as true heroes.

CHAPTER 9

A CLOSER SHAVE WITH DEATH

THE MISCONCEPTION ABOUT GETTING SHOT

Jim saw someone get shot. He knew what it looked like and he knew what to expect. It's not like on television when somebody shoots someone and the victim flies several feet backward onto the ground, or does an acrobatic stunt off of the platform he might be standing on. That's not the case at all. In reality, Jim knew, firsthand, that if someone was shot, you might question as to whether the person was even hit or not, since the person doesn't instantly fall down. When Jim engaged with the first shooting incident in 2002, the criminal had shot first. Jim then engaged in defense, but the man wasn't responding to the shots. Jim thought: *What's going on? Nothing's happening but he's getting shot.* The burglar continued to shoot at Jim even though he had been hit. Finally, Jim delivered a halting shot into the chest, ending the assault.

Media and television sensationalizes shootings, embellishing the victims' reactions to make a riveting story. According to a scientific report, it was revealed that people, who fall down when they are shot, most often do so only because of the psychological effect of it. They associate bullets as being deadly. We have seen it many times in movies where people are shot and fall down or are blown back several feet.

As far as people being launched significantly, due to the force from gunfire, Newton's Third Law defies this phenomenon. If, for any action there is an equal and opposing reaction, the shooter would also have to be thrown in the opposite direction as significantly as the person he shot. Furthermore, the gun would have to have quite some force behind it, to thrust people several feet.

In 2005, a test was conducted with a .50 caliber sniper rifle, a very powerful gun. The experiment was to shoot a dummy that was the size and weight of an average male. After firing, the dummy was only knocked back about two and a half inches.

Usually, a person who gets shot is still ambulant. Matter of fact, someone could get shot and they would still continue to pursue their goal, if they had the mind set to continue doing what they were determined to do. This is even evident in animals. A deer who is shot in the heart often continues running for up to about fifty yards. The animal only collapses, unconscious, due to the loss of blood, not the initial impact from the gun.

If an offender fires his weapon and has resolved, ahead of time, to do something, it doesn't matter if he's shot. He will continue to proceed with what he had predetermined to accomplish until he either fulfills his desires or is incapacitated. During the early twentieth century, American troops, fighting against Moro tribesmen in the Philippines, as well as Boxers in China, discovered, with great astonishment, that their .38 caliber rifles and handguns would not stop a charging enemy. It took as much as four shots to put their adversary down. The enemies became alarmingly impenetrable to bullets, due to their war-fueled adrenaline and their psychological ignorance to the damaging effects of guns.

BY HAPPENSTANCE

On February 25, 2005, a man robbed a bank in Pleasant Grove. He did a hostile takeover where he went in with weapons and commanded everybody to get onto the ground. The workers and customers lives were all at risk as the burglar waved his gun at them, and demanded money. He was already adept at bank holdups, having previously robbed three other banks. He took off in a red Ford Taurus, leaving victims traumatized and shaken. Police officers happen to be in the area at the time of the incident and gave him chase, but lost him through the streets of Pleasant Grove. The police figured he had to be hiding out somewhere nearby, so they searched in their computer system and found some addresses that were potential hide-outs.

Jim had been working that day and he was actually on his way home, since it was the end of his shift. As he drove down a street towards his neighborhood, he noticed several police officers congregating at one particular home. He decided to check things out and see what was going on; perhaps he could be of help.

Jim showed up on scene and recognized some of the officers from surrounding cities. He casually approached them. "Hey what's going on?" he asked. He soon learned, about the robber they were pursuing.

As Jim made his way towards the front door of the house where more police were gathered, an officer from Jim's department went the other way saying "I think the guy's not here. We may as well leave."

Jim said, "Alright." But he thought he should talk to the other guys anyway and find out a little more about the situation.

Jim soon learned that the officers had just barely arrived. They hadn't even gone to the door yet and nobody really knew if the guy was actually there or not. The garage door of the duplex was down and no car was out in front. Also, the house was very quiet, so everything appeared as though it was vacant, but no one was certain. Someone suggested that they go to the door, so one of the officers rang the bell. The sound of locks turned.

"Sounds like he's probably in there," Someone called out.

"That was definitely the front door locking," somebody else commented. "We better get some swat gear." The agents discussed how to get the situation underhand.

Jim stepped back from the front door, where the other officers were discussing what to do next, and turned towards the front of the garage. He observed how the garage doors of the duo housing units were side by side. He drew closer to the garage door belonging to the unit in question and could hear somebody entering into the neighboring garage. It sounded like someone tripping over aluminum cans. "I heard something!" Jim alerted. "Maybe we ought to get someone to pull their car up in front of here in case he tries to back his car out," he suggested. Just then, the garage door in front of him began opening. Jim leaned down and watched it go up, catching sight of the red Ford Taurus, the bandit's car. The garage door continued to go all the way to the top and Jim cautiously stepped to the side where the brick and garage door met. He couldn't see anything, but he could hear somebody rummaging around. He pulled his gun and vigilantly looked for the man. Standing up on the tips of his toes he saw somebody crouching behind the front end of the car opposite of him. Strangely, it appeared that the man was kneeling up against the hood, like he was praying.

"I'm a police officer! Drop your gun and put your hands up!" Jim ordered, ending the criminal's vain prayer.

The man cast a glance at Jim as if to say, "Okay, here we go." He stood up and began shooting at Jim.

Jim lunged backward, taking cover behind the side wall of the garage, and firing back. The robber started climbing on top of the car as he engaged with Jim. Apparently, there was no other way out of the garage, with a motorcycle on one side of the car, and a large amount of clutter on the other side. The man was otherwise boxed in, so he charged over the car towards Jim, shooting recklessly as he attempted to escape. Jim shot back at the attacker to stop his pursuit, but the shooter was equipped with two 9mm guns, one in each hand, and wouldn't quit. Bullets flew above Jim's head, narrowly missing him and severely penetrating the sheetrock behind him. Although the man had been hit by Jim's fire, it wasn't until the guy was nearly to the edge of the car, and less than five feet away, when Jim delivered a final shot to the thief's head. Jim had no other choice. The bank robber collapsed on top of the Ford Taurus and the pursuit was over.

Jim went in the next day for interviews concerning the investigation. During the shooting he had tunnel vision, being completely focused on the gunman and the aggressive assault. During the attack, Jim felt as though time had slowed down so he could key in on the bandit. He hadn't seen the bullet bike motorcycle on the side of the car, which had been purchased with the money the robber had previously stolen from banks. He didn't see the clutter and debris on the other side of the car, forcing the man to climb over the vehicle to flee, and he certainly didn't see that the offender had two 9mm semi-automatic Glocks. He only saw the shooter climbing over the car, charging towards him.

It was miraculous that Jim didn't get hit at all; he was only about five feet away when the bandit was at his closest. Jim recalled the bullet that buzzed the top of his head. Bullet holes from the man's gun were not only found throughout the garage drywall, but also on the Ford Taurus. It was a miracle that no one else got injured.

What was most astounding to Jim was how the man continued to go over the car, even though he had been hit several times. It wasn't until the thief was incapacitated that he finally quit firing.

I WAS THERE

Years later, when Jim went to his high school reunion, he learned that one of the victims during the bank robbery was a guy he went to school with. The guy approached Jim and revealed to him the details. "I was working there at the bank when it happened. The robber came in and he made us get down on the ground. It was that same robber that you stopped." His classmate's words surprised Jim. It put an intimate perspective on that incident, as well as every case he was involved with. It wasn't only about keeping the community safe; it was also about protecting his friends and family, people he knew and loved. Every day, people are involved in accidents and you feel bad for them, but when it's people you know, it affects you in a very personal way.

CHAPTER 10

GONE QUICKLY

There may come a time in everyone's life when they realize how fragile life really is, and how precious time spent together can be. Death is usually the deliverer of such a rude awakening. As people you are acquainted with, whether family, friends, or casual associations, cross over the line from human mortal existence, you suddenly merge into the startling understanding of the life we sometimes take for granted.

In some incidents that Jim dealt with during his career, he witnessed how quickly somebody can go and how devastating it is to the people who know and love them.

DEATH AT THE CROSSROADS

Where highways 73 and 68 intersect in Saratoga, they call it the *Crossroads*. There were two lanes running in both directions of the remote road, and the speed limit was 60 mph. It wasn't unusual for accidents to occur on such a dangerous road. Jim got called to respond to an accident where a vehicle was t-boned at these crossroads.

One young kid, about 14 years old, was thrown from his vehicle into a field off the side of the road. The streets had been closed off and the intersection suddenly became a parking lot for emergency vehicles and personnel.

When Jim arrived, he saw the teen-aged boy lying comfortably in the grass. Although injured, he appeared to be fine. Jim even engaged in a conversation with the young man and marveled at how alert he was. Jim watched as he was placed in the ambulance and taken to the hospital to be checked out. The two intersecting roads eventually opened up again, and Jim continued with the responsibilities of his day.

A couple hours later, Jim got word that the kid from the Crossroads accident had died. Jim was stunned. Things seemed okay but apparently they weren't as good as he thought. It was hard for Jim to process. He had just spoken with this boy. One minute he was alive, and less than two hours later, he was gone, that quick. It impressed deeply upon Jim how life should never be taken for granted.

JEEP FUN

One Saturday afternoon, Jim pulled up to a gas station to get a soda. He noticed some young guys at the pump in a Jeep without a top on, and he was a little concerned. These kids were in their twenties and leaving to have some fun. Jim hoped they would keep their heads straight and not do anything crazy. The kids headed up a road towards Eagle Mountain.

Jim walked into the convenience store, bought his soda and then returned to his patrol car. He sat for a moment, to enjoy his drink and take a little break. Finally, he headed out to patrol the streets of Lehi.

Nearly an hour later, he heard sirens. Jim's heart sunk; for the very reason he dreaded. It was the kids in the jeep. Apparently their vehicle couldn't make it up the hill. The jeep tipped over, rolled onto one of the kids, and killed him. They were just going to have fun. Jim was spooked, recalling how he had seen them only an hour earlier, alive and laughing. Now their lives were changed and one of them was dead.

SIDS

In Pleasant Grove Jim went on a medical call for a baby who was not breathing. When he arrived, he discovered a small infant had died in her crib. They determined it was SIDS: Sudden Infant Death Syndrome. The mother, who was devastated, had attested that everything was just fine when she laid the baby down for a nap. She left and came back a short time later and found the child wasn't breathing.

Jim pondered deeply how things could be fine one minute and then suddenly, that's it. They're gone. It was kind of bizarre.

A WANTED KID

There was a kid in Pleasant Grove that Jim and his department used to deal with quite regularly. Everybody knew who he was. He'd been arrested dozens of times and was wanted for warrants, drugs or anything else that was possible to be wanted for. He was just one of those kids whom every police officer was familiar with, but wasn't exactly annoyed by. This kid somehow acquired a street bike. One day he was zipping down Geneva road, when he lost control and hit a tree. He was killed instantly. Jim wasn't called to the scene, but the kid's death really moved him. The boy was somebody he saw on a regular basis and was almost like a friend. It was strange to Jim, to know someone and deal with him almost daily, and then realize you wouldn't see him again in this life.

COOPER

About a year before Jim retired, he was called to a home where a child was run over by a vehicle. The boy's name was Cooper and he was only about 5 years old. He had been swimming outside on a hot summer day, and went to the end of the warm driveway to dry off in the sun.

Cooper's aunt got into her suburban, which was parked in the carport close to the house. The drive way was unusually long and Cooper was about 20 yards beyond the main carport. When the aunt pulled out of the carport, to leave, she unknowingly backed over the top of her nephew, killing him instantly.

When Jim got there, Cooper was still in the driveway. The aunt had pulled a little bit forward so the boy was no longer underneath the vehicle. She had run over the top of his head, creating a gruesome sight amidst an emotional tragedy. Jim got some blankets and laid them over the small body so he wasn't exposed. Seeing the small child lying dead underneath the covering and watching the family weeping over the accident truly put things into perspective. One minute the kid was out swimming under the sun, laughing and having a good time. The next minute, burial plans were being made. Jim's heart sunk.

CHAPTER 11

UNORTHODOX EXPECTATIONS

24 HOURS A DAY

On television, the police are often depicted as working a typical 9 to 5 shift, beginning their day with a casual beverage in the morning. The day accelerates into a high adventure case, which results in a chase and then a shoot out. By the end of the day, they solve the case and clock out, heading towards the bar before going home. Everything is fine when they go to bed, and they wake up the next morning, new and refreshed, only to repeat the same routine with a slightly different adventure to satisfy the next television episode.

In reality, police officers don't have shootouts every day, they don't return back to work the next morning feeling refreshed as though nothing happened the day before, and they don't work a normal 9 to 5 shift. They deal with a range of issues that are emotionally and physically wearing and they work various shifts ranging from 10 to 12 hours a day, covering every hour around the clock. Protecting the people is an endless responsibility, shared between the officers of each police department. About every two months, Jim rotated between shifts consisting of the day shift from 7am to 5 p.m., the swing shift from 3 p.m. to 1 a.m., and grave yard from 9 p.m. to 7 a.m. Occasionally Jim would work 12 hr shifts from 6 to 6, called "twelves". For about half a year, he did these *twelves* with the department. Days off were also inconsistent with the norm. Jim would work alternate rotations of weekends and week days. Additionally, there was time spent in court. Sometimes, when Jim would work a grave yard shift, he would get off at 7 in the morning then have to go to court at 9 or 10 a.m. Court lasted anywhere from a half an hour to three hours. Then Jim would go home and try to get some sleep so he could go back out again at 9pm to work another *graveyard*. It was hard.

Combining the erratic work schedule with little sleep and

high-stress, definitely puts strain on the body. An inconsistent scheduling, alone, is enough to put most people off balance. The average person doesn't sleep all day and stay up all night. The body just doesn't manage well under those circumstances.

The circadian rhythm is a biological 24-hour cycle of body processes, also known as an internal body clock. Light and darkness primarily affect the body clock, determining when a body releases certain chemicals in order to function normally. When circadian rhythms are disrupted or altered, sleep patterns, hormone release, blood pressure, body temperature, and other bodily functions are influenced. Although the circadian rhythm is built into our systems, environmental factors can adjust our body clock. Work shifts that don't coincide with the natural schedule of the sunlight, such as night or graveyard shifts, are among the biggest factors that contribute to a disruption in biological rhythms. Rotating 24-hour shifts are the worst, due to the inconsistency of a person's exposure to sunlight. A prolonged disturbance of rhythms can result in disorders.

People, who have careers that require working around the clock on a rotating cycle rather than a fixed pattern, have an extremely high risk of acquiring diseases such as depression, type 2 diabetes, bipolar disorder, insomnia and obesity. Additionally, a person's ability to be alert, and maintain body temperature can be affected as well as their appetite and hormone secretion.

Certainly, men and women working in law enforcement are subject to the strenuous wear and tear that their career places on them physically, mentally, and emotionally. Nevertheless, they are determined to submit to these harsh factors in order to serve their communities.

MELANIE'S TASK

It was especially difficult for Jim to sleep during the day when there were little ones at home. Melanie tried to keep them quiet while her husband was resting, but it wasn't easy. She would whisper to the children to keep their voices down so they wouldn't wake Daddy up. Melanie's whispers would become louder and louder, as the children grew louder. But, often times, it was her voice telling the kids to be quiet that woke Jim up, not the children. He would groggily stagger into the living room and squint at Melanie with a questioning expression. She would just shrug and say, "Sorry, I'm trying. The kids...you know..." Jim would nod, pulling a tolerant half-grin and stumble back to bed.

Equally challenging to the initial task of sleeping while the family was awake, was Jim's inability of sleeping deeply. He slept lightly because, as a police officer, his mind was programmed to be alert and cautious, causing his shallow sleeping condition.

STRESS OF THE EXTREME KIND

Every task an officer deals with on a daily basis is stressful, by any human standard. Some events are instantly traumatizing, such as threats, assaults, aggravated assaults, chases, weapon confrontations and shootouts. While other less threatening incidents such as making traffic stops, issuing citations, testifying in court, responding to low key calls, enforcing the law, and patrolling areas they are assigned to, are accumulatively taxing. There isn't time to recover from every distressing incident, and often a police officer must go from one demanding moment to the next without any consideration of his own emotions.

When a person feels a threat of any kind, the body has a natural ability to release stress hormones that cause physical changes in the body including heightened blood pressure, increased heart rate, quickened breath, and sharpened senses. These changes naturally prepare the body to fight or flee in a perilous situation, which can prove beneficial for one's escape from a troublesome event. However, prolonged stress or a stress overload can be seriously injurious, leading to physical and mental problems. It can also put unnecessary strain on relationships and impair personal performance. Additionally detrimental, stress can cause a person to become acclimatized to the discomfort it brings, not recognizing when they, personally, have become out of control and in need of seeking professional help.

It's normal for someone not to recognize how stress is affecting them. There is a great tendency for a person to brush off his or her feelings or to ignore issues which are usually deemed by society as insignificant. But if a person continues to neglect their emotional and mental health, just like any spectrum concerning the human body, it could be dangerously debilitating. If stress isn't resolved, it can lead to heart attacks, strokes, depression, anxiety, autoimmune diseases, and other health problems. It can place people against a wall until they explode like a time bomb. Finally, the more a body's stress system is triggered, the more difficult it becomes to shut overloading stress cues down.

People deal with stress in many different ways. Some options of coping actually compound the problem. Eating comfort food, drinking too many alcoholic beverages, watching television, engaging too long on the computer, or taking pills to relax might not be the healthiest way to respond to stress. There are better solutions to managing stress by setting aside time to meditate, exercising regularly, eating healthy, and getting proper sleep.

Unfortunately, not all lifestyles accommodate healthy solutions when dealing with stress. With a demanding, high-risk occupation, coupled with unrelenting work schedules, police officers don't have the most ideal circumstances to manage stress. Many law enforcement workers suffer from physical, emotional, and mental repercussions due to their extremely inclement line of work. Mental health for police officers is a serious matter. Suicides among police officers have increased dramatically over the last few years. Some larger police departments have adopted suicide intervention and mental health programs, resulting in the decline of suicides and improvement of the employees' overall well being.

Regardless of the challenges that a police officer must face, courageous men and women fearlessly pursue this extreme career. Certainly, it takes someone quite extraordinary.

NOT AS IT SEEMS

Jim had a secretary at work whose son wanted to go into criminal justice to be a Crime Scene Investigator just like on the television show, CSI. He was entranced by the glamour that Hollywood depicted of the seemingly glorified career.

"Not everything works out the way it is on television," Jim advised the secretary. "Tell your son that if he really wants to know what it's like to be a CSI, take him up to the crime lab one day and meet with the doctors that do medical exams and autopsies, because that's what it's really like. There is a lot more involved, like collecting physical evidence from bodies. It stinks, it's foul, and it's not going to have all the glory you think it does."

Jim never had to be involved with a high profile case, but

even with the small cases he encountered, he understood what the front line investigators were dealing with. They managed so many things coming in from so many different directions. A great deal of time and money was invested in the actual investigations, and cases weren't solved overnight. Television put a terrible spin on investigations, giving the illusion that mysteries were solved by the end of the day. But in real life, things didn't work that way.

Just before he retired, Jim dealt with a homicide in Orem, and it took a couple months just to get the evidence analyzed by an expert. Jim thought about the case involving Susan Powell. The investigators were working with some difficult factors including a body that they didn't know of its whereabouts, and a husband who automatically got an attorney but wasn't going to talk. They were dealing with a missing person case or a murder from ground zero, questioning if Susan really was out in the West Desert. Additionally, the siblings of the husband were fighting over the money, admitting that their brother did kill his wife just so they could claim the inheritance. All-in-all, investigating was very tedious, stressful, and took a lot of patience.

CIVIL RIGHTS VS. JUSTICE

There are cases where guilty people are getting away with their crimes. You could have the most rock solid case where you could convict somebody without a shadow of a doubt, but if you crossed the line of violating their civil rights, there would be lawyers swarming all over it, and you just lost the entire case over civil rights.

A long time ago, the defense attorney's job was to defend someone who was innocent. Today, it's not necessarily about defending the innocent but, rather, trying to find fault with the law so the guilty can evade punishment. All it takes is a little clause here or a small loophole there, and the criminal goes free. Some radicals and activists are just looking for an argument or some avenue to give them license to do whatever they want. They attempt to redefine the laws to obtain a goal based on an extremely liberal opinion. Nevertheless, it seems as though the constitution is constantly being challenged, and the rights of innocent people are becoming lost in the contorted views of selfish objectives.

CHAPTER 12

SUICIDES

Jim had been on numerous calls involving suicides, and the varying range of victims often surprised him. Jim felt that suicides always had a strange feeling about them.

THE ELDERLY

The oldest person he got called to, for a suicide, was an old lady who wasn't very well. She spent most of her time, sick in bed. Jim was still fairly new in the police force, and this was one of his first suicides. When he arrived, he discovered that she had used a small caliber pistol and shot herself in the head.

THE YOUNG

When Jim first started in Orem, he got called to a home where a kid had shot himself with a gun. He was in his house and simply went downstairs and shot himself. His family kind of knew that the boy was having troubles, and they could see things leading up to it, but it was completely unexpected for him to end his life.

Often people are aware when their family members are having difficulties because they are on drugs, depressed, or sick. But, often, the family doesn't know how to help, or doesn't realize how severe the problem has become. Sometimes, a specific event will trigger a suicide. Unfortunately, hind sight is always much clearer.

TROUBLED WIFE, IRRATIONAL HUSBAND

Once Jim was working in Pleasant Grove and he was called to a home where the wife had taken a pill and killed herself. The husband had found her and called the police. Because of the nature of the incident, the police had to get the husband out of the house to do the investigation, especially since he was automatically a suspect. The man insisted on going into the house, but they couldn't comply. The man even threatened to punch Jim because he wouldn't let him in the house. Another officer tried to reason with the man, and get him to calm down while they did the on-scene investigation, but the man was out of control and reacting irrationally. Jim understood that there was an emotional side the man was dealing with, but he was well over the top, making it difficult for Jim and the other officers and investigators to do their job.

HOOKING A HOSE UP

Jim was dispatched to a street where a man was exhibiting peculiar behavior in his car. The person, who made the call to dispatch, explained the nature of the man's odd behavior. "A guy's out in his car and he's doing something strange," she began. "Oh, now he's hooking a hose up to the window..."

Jim and his partner responded to the scene and located the man in his car. Sure enough, there was a hose hooked to the window from the exhaust pipe, and the car was running. Jim could see the man sitting in his car, with absolutely no clothes on. Jim and his partner knocked on the window and the man rolled it down.

"What are you doing?" Jim asked in astonishment.

"Nothing," the man answered. "I'm not doing anything."

Jim scrunched his brow. "What do you mean you're not doing anything? You need to get some clothes on, then we'll take you to get some help." Jim and his partner escorted the man to his house to get dressed, and then took him to the hospital to see a psychiatrist. This was the first person he came across who tried to asphyxiate himself and was in the process of doing it when he arrived. It was more common to come across a victim, who was already dead, or one who was threatening he was going to do it, but not often did he confront someone who was in the middle of it.

AN ENDING IN THE GARAGE

Jim was called to a home where a man killed himself with a gun. He had been in the house and there was an argument. The wife left the house because he was in a rage, and he took off into the garage. She called the police saying, "My husband's got a gun and he went into the garage with it."

When Jim and his partner arrived, they discovered that the woman had thought she heard the gun fire, but she wasn't sure. Jim called for the man but there was no answer. "Okay." Jim glanced at his partner. "We're going to have to go in and look." They went into the garage and found the man. He had already shot himself before they had gotten there. Jim sadly viewed the scene, recognizing the man.

About a week or two earlier, the man was having one of his anxiety episodes and he was out in the shed. Jim and his partner went to the house and found that he had cut himself terribly. They called for an ambulance and took him to the hospital to get psychiatric help as well as medical attention.

Only a couple weeks later, Jim was at the same house again, but this would be the last time.

DEATH IN THE BACKYARD

There was one incident where Jim and his partner got called to a house where a man was threatening suicide. When Jim arrived at the house, the wife exclaimed that her husband had a gun, and he just barely ran into the backyard. Jim and the other officer went down the side of the house, unsure of the man's intentions. There had been a family fight and Jim didn't want to run back there without checking things out first, knowing the man was armed. Cautiously, he peaked around the corner. As he peered into the backyard, he spotted the man sitting against the back of the house. He had already shot himself, just minutes before Jim and his partner had arrived. It happened that quickly. As Jim approached the man, he could tell he was already dead. The other officer thought that maybe he was still alive, because the incident was so fresh. He had, at first, thought that there was a chance that they could save him. But soon, it was evident that the man was dead and not revivable.

CHAPTER 13

ODDS AND ENDS

A RATTLING DOORKNOB

Not only did Jim live on the edge as a police officer, but he also slept on the edge, unable to acquire deep sleep. It was how Jim's mind worked. It came with instinctively being cautious, always listening for the smallest things. He could hear sounds unlike the average person. It was almost as if he was trying to pay attention but trying to sleep at the same time, like sleeping with one eye open. But there was one time where Jim did sleep deep, and, ironically, it happened during one of the most bizarre incidents that occurred at his home.

Jim and his family were living in an apartment while he was working for the Pleasant Grove police department. It was around 7 in the morning and he had just returned home from working all night. After eating dinner, he retired to bed. Melanie drove their twins to school then returned home. The youngest, Casey, was only three, giving Melanie the challenge of keeping him entertained quietly while Jim slept. Casey loved to lock and unlock doors, and he was fascinated with the power of doorknobs. After all, they opened doors.

Melanie was on the phone with Jim's mom, just talking about random everyday things. She heard the door knob rattle, but didn't pay any attention to it since Casey was standing near the front door, which was locked. She figured it was him.

But Casey wasn't playing with the knob. When he heard the rattling, he reached over and unlocked the door. All of a sudden, the door flew open and a man crawled in. Melanie gasped. She yelled, "I gotta go" on the phone and hung up with her mother-in-law. Afterward, she thought: *That was a dumb thing to do. I should have kept her on the phone in a situation like this.*

Quickly, she snatched up Casey and retreated back. She didn't know who this man was and why he was crawling into her home. She screamed at the top of her lungs, "Get out of my house!"

The man stood up, looking terrified. "Don't call the cops! Don't call the cops!"

Melanie thought: *You wouldn't believe this, but there's one just down the hallway, asleep.* Nevertheless, she didn't reveal her husband's identity to the intruder, fearing what might happen. For all she knew, the man could have a gun and decide to run through the house until he found Jim, and then shoot him in his sleep. Obviously, he wasn't aware that the home he chose to find refuge in was the home of a person he was trying to evade. There wasn't any evidence that a police officer lived there, especially since the patrol car was parked in the back of the apartments.

Melanie continued screaming as loudly as she could for the man to get out, hoping Jim would hear her. When Jim never came, Melanie thought to herself: *Okay, it's not working. Why isn't Jim hearing all this commotion?* Finally, the man agreed to leave and crouched down as he left out the door. Still holding Casey closely, she locked the door behind the man and tore down the hall to the bedroom. "Jim! Jim! Wake up! Someone was in the house!" But Jim remained sound asleep. It took a moment for Melanie to finally stir him, which surprised her. He never slept this deep before, and this was a fine time to do it.

Jim finally woke up, looking more shocked than rested. "Whuh...what's going on?" he asked, groggily.

After Jim learned the details of Melanie's eventful morning, he called down to the department in Orem and discovered their strange guest had just committed a robbery.

The apartment building was a four-plex, and Jim's family lived on the second floor. Jim figured the man had crawled up the stairs from the main level, crouching behind the cement wall along the edge of the building to hide. Then arriving at the Flygare's apartment, he tried the door and Casey let him in.

The police were in the area, but the man just disappeared. Strangely, the suspect was nowhere to be found. Jim didn't think the guy could have gotten away without someone hiding him because there was a large field behind the apartment, and a main road east of them. In broad daylight, somebody would have seen him running. Looking back, Jim wondered if the woman, in the apartment next door to him, had let him in and concealed him with her quirky, hospitality. She was the kind that would have done something like that. He imagined that she invited him to sit down and even asked if he was thirsty, taking pity on the thief as he begged her not to call the cops.

Although they didn't find the man immediately, they had seen him before at the station and knew who he was. Eventually they did locate and arrest him.

TASTE IT

Jim had a situation where he pulled over a man in his early 20's who had stolen a car. As he and the other accompanying officers made the arrest, the thief's mother showed up. Jim and the other officers were searching through the vehicle and found a bottle of pills. Jim pulled the pills out of the car and studied them, curiously. They weren't labeled and they didn't look familiar. He poured a couple in his hand and showed them to the other officers, asking if they knew what they were. As the officers, who were standing next to Jim's left side, discussed the pills, the mother of the suspect in question approached Jim's right side without him knowing.

"What are they?" an officer asked.

"I don't know," another officer answered.

"We need to find out what they are," the first officer commented.

Looking at the pills, Jim jokingly said, "Well, taste one."

To Jim's surprise, the mother grabbed one of the pills from Jim's hand and popped it in her mouth. Jim and the other officers stood gaping. Certainly, Jim didn't count on the woman hearing him, let alone taking him seriously. Fortunately, the pills turned out to be only aspirin.

ALARMED

One time, Jim responded to a junior high school in Lehi where a fire alarm had been pulled. It was in the middle of a Sunday and Jim happened to be alone on shift. He found an open door to the vacated school and entered the building, the alarm still blaring. Searching the dark hallways, he found nobody, but someone had pulled the alarm. It didn't pull itself. With his hand ready to draw his gun, Jim tensely continued his search. After a while, he started to become spooked with the eeriness of it all. He wasn't one to get scared, but searching dark corners while the alarm blasted, caused his imagination to go wild. He was nearly convinced that the *boogie man* was around the corner, ready to pounce on him at any time.

Jim completed his search, finding nobody there. Apparently someone had come into the school, through the open door and pulled the alarm for kicks. It was nerve-racking. Looking back at the incident, Jim realized that, nowadays, he would never go into the building alone because you never know what could await you. But back then, he didn't think it was a problem, other than a mental torment.

ATTACKED BY A ROTTWEILER

A call once came in concerning an aggressive dog, which had posed a threat to nearby neighbors. The animal control was going to check it out, and Jim said he would assist.

Jim was a little apprehensive about responding to the situation, because he wasn't as familiar with animals as he was people. He decided he would bring pepper spray, just in case.

When Jim arrived at the house, he met the animal control officer in front of the home. They walked into the back yard and saw a 120 pound Rottweiler, a sturdy breed standing over two feet high. The history of this breed included being a stock protection dog. They had performed as some of the first police dogs, and also served honorably alongside the military. Nevertheless, in the past ten years, they were responsible for about 73 percent of all canine homicides, possibly due to their cattle-controlling, protective, guard-dog nature. This powerful breed required strict training, and was not to be abused or neglected or it could result in dangerous behavior.

Jim studied the dog, with its large skull and jaws connecting to a neck of nearly solid muscles, and moved further away from the scene. He was thinking: *I don't want to get near that thing.* He felt more comfortable letting the animal control agent take care of it while he observed. It was a different kind of fear that confronted Jim, one that defied his ability to sidestep it so easily. Jim could reason, somewhat, with humans, but dogs were neither as predictable nor rational.

While the animal control attendant cautiously headed towards the dog with his snare pole and police baton, or "bite stick", Jim leaned against the bordering fence at a good distance and placed his finger in position on the pepper spray nozzle. A few curious neighbors watched from the edges of the property. Suddenly, the dog darted towards...Jim.

Watching the powerful canine, viciously charge in his direction, Jim quickly resolved that the pepper spray just might not stop this hostile opponent. He dropped the pepper spray and went for his gun thinking: *Big dog coming at me,* which translated to: *I've got to stop this big dog fast or I'm going to get torn apart.*

Jim shot the dog between the eyes and it went down.

Incidentally, the animal control officer was very relieved. He couldn't believe what he had just witnessed. At the moment the dog ferociously bolted towards Jim, the animal handler rapidly assessed that if it had been him, he wouldn't have reacted so quickly. He had a gun, too, but even if he'd pulled his gun fast enough, he wasn't so sure he would have hit his attacker so accurately, and he may have been severely injured.

The neighbor that called the police about the dog was amazed. He approached Jim saying, "See. I told you that dog was aggressive." He was impressed with Jim's quick actions, and grateful that he no longer had to worry about such a dangerous threat to the neighborhood.

RIDE ALONGS

Melanie went on a few ride-alongs with Jim, where she would join her husband on his street patrols. Sitting in the passenger seat, she observed his work as he pulled over cars for traffic violations. She was impressed at how Jim treated the people with respect, the way he would want to be treated. She watched with intrigue as he approached the vehicles then return to the patrol car, keeping his back to his car and his eye on the driver. He was taught that technique when he first started in the police force. He'd always walk backwards, away from the offender's window, watching to make sure he or she didn't get out of the car or try to drive off. Once he reached his patrol car and got inside, he would write up the report, without being too focused on the paperwork. He'd keep watch on the person in the car simultaneously.

Melanie liked to go on rides with Jim because she was interested in what he did. However, it made Jim nervous because he didn't know what he was going to get into while he was patrolling. He would tell her, "Now if there's something bad, I have to drop you off on the side of the road because you can't take it. And she would think, "Okay, I hope it's not out in the middle of nowhere."

Lehi was okay because it was smaller and there wasn't a lot that was going on in comparison to other, larger cities. At that time, Lehi only had a population of between 10 and 15 thousand people. (Now, at over 54,000 people, Lehi is one of the fastest growing cities in the United States, having ranked number five in 2012.)

Orem, on the other hand, was far bigger. When Jim worked for their police department, it was a little more risky to ride with him. Melanie could understand why Jim didn't really like to take family on ride alongs, because anything could happen.

Melanie remembered a time when she rode with Jim and he received a call that a guy possibly had a knife. Jim had his lights on and tried to hurry to the scene, yet the people driving on the street didn't seem to care. Jim had to weave in and out of traffic to get to the call because people did not want to pull over to allow the emergency vehicles to pass. The Police are trying to hurry to get to a situation to prevent something bad from happening. When citizens didn't pull over to let them by, they were not only disrespectful to the officers, but disrespectful to the citizens that the police were trying to help. Driving with Jim gave Melanie a new perspective of what officers go through.

CHAPTER 14

TALKING ABOUT IT

THE CHILDREN'S REACTION

A couple days after the first shootout Jim had in 2002, he remembered watching television with his family in the evening. Everyone seemed rather quiet, when his youngest son, Casey approached him. Only eight years old, he curiously looked up at his father, who was sitting on the couch next to Melanie, and asked, "Dad, did a bad guy really shoot at you?"

None of his kids seemed interested for the past two days in asking any questions about the incident. Now, Casey was standing in front of him, staring at his father with intrigue. The twins, who were twelve years old, quit watching television and turned their full attention to Jim.

Jim thought for a moment then answered, "Yes, Casey. A

man, who made some bad choices, shot at me. But I am safe, and you're safe, and everything's fine."

The children didn't ask any more questions, or say anything after that. Jim had worried about the kids at school, and whether or not they would get ridiculed or teased. But nothing happened.

Melanie remembers going to the school with Jim's mom after the shooting occurred. They met with the principal and the counselors, who pulled the children out of classes to talk with them. First they let them know that their dad was involved in a shooting. They said he got shot but assured them that he was okay and had only been hit in his arm. Melanie wasn't sure if the children grasped what had happened. She was concerned, especially about Casey. He was so young, and he always took in a whole lot, which always affected him later. He was kind of tender hearted that way. So Melanie and Jim were cautious in saying anything at home about the shooting, and eventually, they got to where it was almost forgotten.

More than ten years later, when Jim and Melanie moved into their new home, Melanie was going through some old school things and came across one of her daughter's school journals. Melanie randomly opened up to a page that her daughter had written. It was dated the day after the shooting. It read, "My dad was involved in a shooting yesterday." It was brief and to the point, but it was a deadening blast from the past. Her daughter didn't say too much, but Melanie realized, at that moment, that the ordeal had been on her daughter's mind, and that she was more aware of the situation than Melanie gave her credit for. She wondered how her daughter had really been feeling, because the kids never said too much about what had happened and never asked a lot of questions, Melanie figured the kids didn't care too much or even understand. But they did and they were listening.

JUST DOING HIS JOB

Another reason, they never discussed the incident at home, was because Jim never wanted to talk about it. He didn't take pride in the fact that he had killed a man. It wasn't about that. Respectively, he was doing his job, protecting the citizens from a man who would steal and kill.

A few years later, Casey did pester his father about sharing some stories, in which Jim would evade him by saying he would tell him when he got older. When Casey turned 20, he confronted his father. "You told me you would tell me your stories when I got older, but you won't." Jim knew exactly what he wanted to hear, but he just didn't like talking about it that way, as if it was a story to brag about. So he didn't say anything. Even among extended family, Jim didn't like to talk about it, and they respected his desire to remain silent. The only things his parents had said when Jim retired was, "Oh, I'm glad you're out of that line of work, because we know you've had some interesting things happen."

There was a crowd he would talk about it with. If other officers asked him about the shootings, he would talk with them if he could see that it would genuinely help them. But outside of law enforcement questioning, Jim kept quiet about it all.

He's had citizens look at his gun and ask, "Oh, you ever shot anybody?" hoping to hear a tale of adventure and bravery. He waves them on and side-sweeps the question. He modestly didn't ever want to boast, or make himself out to be some kind of superhero.

ENDING ON A POSITIVE NOTE

Whenever Jim was involved with an incident and responding to a call, he tried to leave on a good note, regardless of how the situation was affecting him. He was told, early on in his career, that whatever he said, and whatever tone he used when interacting with citizens, they would remember it. If his tone was negative, then the citizens would remember the story as negative. He tried to make sure he bridled his own feelings and dealt professionally and respectfully with every incident.

CONFIDING IN OTHERS

Shortly after the first shooting, Jim went down to Moab to ride dirt bikes with a few of his friends, Michael, Rick, Shawn, and David. He was the only cop among them. After riding for a while, they all took a rest, sitting around a wooden table in a picnic area. Michael was the one who liked to crack jokes. He knew Jim was involved with the first shooting, but the other guys were unaware. They started talking about random things, when someone asked who was the manliest among them. Michael jested, "Jim, because he's shot the most people." Jim didn't say anything. Rick gave Jim a peculiar look and said, "Yeah, whatever." Things like that didn't happen where they lived and the guys were all convinced that Michael was teasing Jim because he was a police officer. Jim preferred to let them believe it was only a joke.

The only reason Michael knew, was because of a dirt biking trip that he and Jim took previously in Cherry Creek. They were coming home and started talking about Jim's job.

Michael harassed Jim, asking, "You ever shot anybody?" He had bugged Jim before on past trips. Finally, coming home from Cherry Creek, Jim answered, "Well, yeah, I did."

At first Michael didn't process it, and then he gave Jim a peculiar look. "You had to shoot a dog, right? Is that what you're talking about?" He was referring to the Rottweiler.

"Yeah, I shot a dog," Jim answered, seriously. "But that's not what I'm saying. I shot a man. I had to." Although Michael appeared stunned, Jim went on, filling him in about the shoot off he had with Ricardo in 2002. Since then, Michael never teased Jim about it again, until the one time in Moab.

One of Jim's really good friends, Brandon Harvey, understood a little bit more about him. The two had been acquaintances for over 30 years and had known each other since high school. Brandon was aware of the shooting, but he never brought it up. Jim didn't, so, respectfully, he didn't either.

After the second shooting occurred, Jim's biking friends learned quickly about both incidents, instilling a sense of startling reality in them. But he still didn't talk with them about it.

Jim recognized that it was important to work through his feelings and emotions when something was bothering him, but he had to find a certain person to vent to or else it would backfire. Some people make things out to be bigger than you explained it, misjudge your actions, or downplay the situation, making you feel like your emotions were insignificant and you were overreacting. Sometimes it was a personality clash. So Jim carefully chose people he knew he could confide in whenever he shared information.

Jim had heard of large police departments that had full time psychiatrists who worked for them. Early on, he thought it was silly. But after working in the field for a short while, he immediately understood why they invested so wisely.

NOT ONCE BUT TWICE

Once Jim was talking with his sergeant about the first shooting he was involved with. He asked, "Could you do it, Sarge? Could you actually engage in shooting with someone? Maybe you could do it once. But there's the second one I was involved in. Could you do it again like I did?" It posed a deeper question that the sergeant wasn't sure he could answer right away. Perhaps only experience could really dictate the true answer for every individual.

Jim was well aware of the emotions he faced immediately after the first shooting and the self-doubt he experienced. At times, he wondered if his feelings would escalate to the point where he couldn't pull his gun again because he was too overwhelmed or scared. He remembered going to the range afterward and becoming a little anxious just shooting the gun for the first time since the incident. He also suffered, on occasion, from nightmares about guns that didn't shoot and gang retaliation. But Jim didn't give up. He was determined to get back on course. He believed that if he redeveloped his mind set again, then he could do it again. And he was right. Little did he know that in less than three years, he would engage, for the second time, in another shootout.

CHAPTER 15

UNDENIABLE MIRACLES

Throughout the 20 years that Jim served in law enforcement, he witnessed phenomenal occurrences that were nothing less than miracles. Things happened that defied the odds and were highly impractical to science. Jim's life was spared many times, and events seemed to align themselves inexplicably. He and his wife, undoubtedly, agree that many miracles took place during Jim's tenure as a police officer.

THE FIRST SHOOTING

When the first shooting occurred, the thief began the engagement, continuously shooting over his shoulder with his back to Jim at close range. The thief and Jim were less than five feet apart, and yet Jim only suffered a muzzle blast to his arm. Muzzle blast occurs within a foot away from the firearm, which meant Jim was standing within muzzle blast range. Something had to be blocking Jim, protecting him from getting hit. It could be argued that the thief was a terrible shot, especially shooting over his shoulder. But at that close range, it was near impossible for him to shoot so many bullets without at least one hitting Jim. You can still see on Jim's police jacket, the singed nylon fabric surrounding the hole where it was grazed, proving the close proximity of the shootout.

Another miracle, that might be overlooked, was the fact that when the ambulance drove away, snow began to fall. Amazingly enough, snow wasn't present before or during the chase, which might have created slippery surfaces, and an even more perilous outcome.

And yet, a third miracle occurred with this incident, involving Sergeant Ron Carlson. There was one point where he had to decide which way to chase the bandit. If he went one way, it would put him safely behind the pursuit, in which Jim would be the one engaging with the robber. If Sergeant Carlson took the other direction, which had been his first instinct, he would have met the armed robber head on, and had been the one to intercept the shooting. For some unexplained reason, the sirens and lights to Jim's patrol car turned on by themselves while Jim was chasing the offender. This caused Sergeant Carlson to head towards the patrol car, putting him on the safer path behind Jim and the suspect. Neither of the officers knew that the burglar was packing a gun, but Jim's quick reactive thought process enabled him to instantaneously pull his gun and shoot back. Sergeant Carlson didn't think he'd be so quick to defend himself if he had confronted the perpetrator face to face. Certainly, the outcome would have been different for Sergeant Carlson. Still, to this day, Jim doesn't know what caused the sirens to sound.

SECOND SHOOTING

Previous to the second shooting, Jim was supposed to go home for the day because it was the end of his shift. Instead, for some reason, he headed down the street to a home where other officers were congregating to determine if a bank robber was hiding there. Jim happened to stop at the house and ask about the situation, and he happened to be the one who moved in front of the garage where he would be directly in line to engage with a shooter that was armed with two guns. It was Jim's skillful shot that ended the attacker's pursuit.

Additionally, Jim was approximately ten feet away when the thief first started shooting at him. The robber climbed up and over the car towards Jim, continuously shooting, until he was only five feet away. The shooter had two guns and yet, somehow, Jim was unharmed. Not a single bullet hit him. Jim still remembered the one bullet that barely buzzed over his head, hitting the drywall behind him. It was a miracle that nobody else was injured. There were several bullet holes in the drywall of the garage, as well as in the roof of the car.

GANGS ON STATE STREET

Some miracles begin to formulate well before they fully reveal themselves. When Jim had pulled a car over on State Street, four gang members were in the car. Jim happened to know the driver, Cal. Jim had previously become acquainted with Cal because he was regularly getting into trouble with the law. Developing a good rapport with Cal was a blessing that would prove valuable. Because of the good rapport, Cal divulged to Jim that there was a gun in the car during the State Street pullover. Jim was able to call for backup before checking the car, preventing a possibly fateful scenario.

Some people don't believe in miracles, despite the undeniable evidence. Jim is certain there is no other explanation for so many instances when his life, and others' lives, were spared.

CHAPTER 16

RETIREMENT

After 20 years of public safety service, Jim retired in March of 2013. He was never sued with any of the incidents he was involved with, although the chances of getting sued with shootings are very high, and almost certain. He was cleared from both shootings, as attorneys ruled the act as self-dense. Jim did what had to be done under perilous circumstances. No officer wants to be faced with what Jim experienced. He served honestly, respectfully, and with great devotion and zeal. As a dedicated police officer, he never received a formal reprimand. He wasn't perfect, and there were times he had been told not to do minor things, just like anyone else, but he was never written up and never received formal discipline. He gleaned important skills from comrades and leaders surrounding him in his work field and performed with precision and respect.

AWARDS

During his time as an officer, Jim was presented by the Chief of Police, two Distinguished Service Citation Awards, honoring him on two separate occasions, for being a public safety hero.

In addition to receiving Officer of the Month a few times, he also received a Letter of Commendation and a prestigious plaque from the city of Lehi for his heroism in discovering a fire and saving the lives and home of an elderly couple.

Jim also received two Letters of Commendation for two separate accounts in finding burglars. On the first occasion, Jim was alerted of a stereo theft. During that day, Jim happened to be driving through the parking lot of the University Mall in Orem. He spotted a suspicious car, which happened to belong to the suspect in question and, ultimately, captured the burglar.

The second incident happened when Jim was patrolling the streets of Orem, during the day, and noticed two juveniles possessing backpacks. Jim pulled up next to the truant youth, who were sitting on the lawn in front of a house. Jim asked the teenagers, who happened to be junior high school students, if they lived at that house. The teens said no. Jim asked why they weren't in school and if he could see inside their backpacks. The teens couldn't reasonably answer why they were skipping school and told the officer that he could not look in their belongings. Knowing that the kids were supposed to be in school, and under the rules of the district, he obtained permission from the school administration to approve the investigation of their packs since it was during school hours. Ironically, the junior high had been experiencing a rash of burglaries during the past few weeks. When Jim searched the boys' possessions, he discovered stolen property they had taken from the school. The boys were later identified as the thieves responsible for all the recent school burglaries, and were arrested.

When Jim retired, he was the only officer, at that time, to have been involved in two combat shootings in Utah County. There was a sniper in the specialized services that had been shot at twice, but he had not been engaging with someone else.

EXTRAORDINARY

Police officers serve the public, ensuring the protection and well-being of the citizens. They maintain the law, prevent crime, and perform an endless list of tasks and responsibilities under implausibly demanding conditions. For Jim, he's learned to see it as just another day on the job, regardless of how challenging and laborious it may be. It takes an extraordinary person to be a police officer and to have accomplished what Jim has. Perhaps that was why he followed the career path he did, utilizing the gifts and skills he was blessed with to protect people and improve their quality of life. Certainly, he knows what kind of courage it takes to be on the other side of a Glock.

ABOUT JIM

Jim was raised in Orem, Utah. He loves hunting, fishing, riding dirt bikes, and watching rodeos. He likes to have his kids involved in whatever he is doing, even if it's just going for a ride somewhere. Now He has one grandchild and likes to include her with family activities. When he goes fishing he tries to get everybody to go, but that doesn't always work out. So, Jim resorts to just having the kids over for dinner and hanging around.

After retirement, Jim went straight to Rio Tinto, Kennecott Copper Mine. He left there to work for Hadco Construction but he missed the line of work he had become accustomed to for 20 years. He was hired by the Department of Commerce in July of 2014 to work as an Investigator, where he is currently employed.

JIM'S TIMELINE

March 1990: Married Melanie.

March 1991: Started police academy, taking evening classes while he worked full time at Nu-Skin International.

February 1992: Graduated from Police Academy.

November 1992: First Job at the Utah State Prison as a Correctional Officer. His Friend, Tony Barton, pointed him in this direction to get his first badge. He worked as a block officer while he waited for a job as a police officer.

September 1993: Started working for Lehi Police Department.

August 1996: Started working for Pleasant Grove Police Department.

March 2001-2013: Worked for Orem Police Department.

March 2013: Retired.

Other Positions and Training: Firearms Instructor, Instructor development, CIT (Crisis Intervention Team). To achieve these positions, Jim utilized the training in which he had to have 40 hours every year, as did every officer, to maintain his POST Certification. He also obtained his Mid Management certificate.

THOUGHTS FROM MELANIE

Having a husband as a police officer was hard. Jim didn't really talk about his experiences. He always separated home from work. He was excited to become a police officer, finally doing what he always wanted to do. But nobody knew what was to come. He survived two shootings and made a difference in many people's lives.

I think Jim has been a lot more relaxed since his retirement. There has been a lot more time to spend with family. We have had barbecues up Provo Canyon together and other fun activities. Jim loves to spend as much time with the family as he can. Sometimes it's hard to get together when everyone is doing their own thing. But our family had an opportunity to go to the National Finals Rodeo in December of 2013 and had a lot of fun. The older children didn't go, and I wish they would have, but that's how it is when families grow and move on.

Sometimes Jim longs for the days when the children were younger and they would go for their long rides as a family. Sometimes they would drive to Bryce Canyon and back, in one day. It was a long, fun day, and they enjoyed special times like that. It would be nice to do it again. If they had a bus, they would all load up and head somewhere together, anywhere to make a happy memory.

It's my greatest hope for this book to help others who might be going through the same emotions as me, having a husband being a police officer, or being involved in a shooting and living through it. If sharing his life experiences with others would make a difference, it would be well worth telling the stories that were seldom told.

CITES:

1. http://vcp.e2bn.org/justice/page11377-the-development-of-a-police-force.html
2. http://en.wikipedia.org/wiki/History_of_law_enforcement_in_the_United_Kingdom
3. http://en.wikipedia.org/wiki/Law_enforcement
4. http://www.nleomf.org/museum/news/newsletters/online-insider/2012/April-2012/early-days-american-law-enforcement-april-2012.html
5. http://plsonline.eku.edu/insidelook/history-policing-united-states-part-1
6. http://en.wikipedia.org/wiki/Police
7. http://www.abrahamlincolnonline.org/lincoln/speeches/house.htm
8. *The New Testament of our Lord and Savior Jesus Christ*, Book of Matthew, April 1997 United States, Quebecor Printing
9. http://en.wikipedia.org/wiki/List_of_civil_wars
10. https://www.childwelfare.gov/pubs/factsheets/domesticviolence.cfm Carlson, B. E. (2000). Children exposed to intimate partner violence: Research findings and implications for intervention. TRAUMA, VIOLENCE, AND ABUSE, 1(4), pp. 321 to 340.
11. http://www.realclearscience.com/blog/2013/07/why-do-people-fall-down-when-shot.html *Stiff: The Curious Lives of Human Cadavers,* Mary Roach, 2004)
12. http://www.dogsbite.org/dog-bite-statistics-fatalities-2012.php
13. http://www.helpguide.org/articles/stress/stress-symptoms-causes-and-effects.htm
14. http://www.ksl.com/?nid=148&sid=30002064
15. https://portal.chicagopolice.org/portal/page/portal/ClearPath/News/Statistical%20Reports/Annual%20Reports/10AR.pdf
16. http://www.ksl.com/?sid=36449335&nid=148&title=police-demonstration-illustrates-danger-of-high-risk-traffic-stops
17. http://www.bountifulcitypd.com/about-us
18. https://en.wikipedia.org/wiki/Ferguson_unrest
19. https://en.wikipedia.org/wiki/Shooting_of_Michael_Brown
20. http://www.crimeinamerica.net/2010/09/29/percent-of-released-prisoners-returning-to-incarceration/
21. http://journalistsresource.org/studies/government/criminal-justice/police-reasonable-force-brutality-race-research-review-statistics
22. http://publicsafety.utah.gov/bci/documents/Crime_In_Utah_2012.pdf
23. https://www.ksl.com/?sid=24544816

Award winning playwright, Sherry Allred is an author, composer, director, producer, SEO writer, public speaker, actress, wife, mother and grandmother. She attended the University of Utah and has written three other novels. She is the writer, composer, director, and producer of a full-length musical, *Nephi and the Sword of Laban*. She has also directed several smaller productions and plays.

Learn more on **www.sherryallred.com.**

Made in the USA
Monee, IL
25 September 2020

42610036R00105